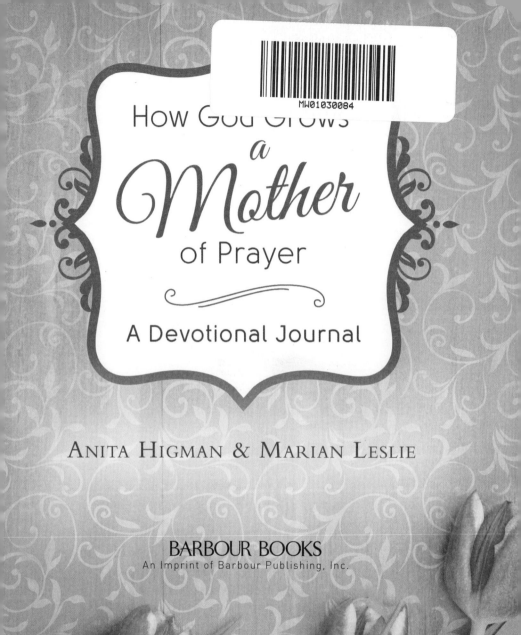

How God Grows
a
Mother
of Prayer

A Devotional Journal

ANITA HIGMAN & MARIAN LESLIE

BARBOUR BOOKS
An Imprint of Barbour Publishing, Inc.

Our mission is to publish and distribute inspirational products offering exceptional value and biblical encouragement to the masses.

Member of the
Evangelical Christian
Publishers Association

Printed in China.

Dedication

To all the mother prayer warriors,
who bravely go to God's throne every
day on behalf of their children.
Your faith grows mine.
Thank you!
—Marian Leslie

To Denise L. Sturgeon.
This world is a finer place
because of your generosity,
your kindness, and
your heart for prayer.
Thank you for being you!
—Anita Higman

Introduction

Motherhood is made up of thousands of little "Mom Moments." What may seem like mere routine chores and happenings—such as cooking a meal, fixing a boo-boo, driving to a guitar lesson, reading a bedtime story, drying a tear, tying a shoelace, or whispering words of love—turn out to be part of a much bigger life picture. God can take what feels like mundane tasks and turn them into the miracle of a beautiful garden of humanity. Helping to grow a child into a young man or woman who follows the Lord and knows the unique gifts he or she has to offer the world is a most glorious profession.

Motherhood is one of the most essential, challenging, satisfying, and beautiful occupations on earth. But for certain, all of those moments spent cultivating, nurturing, protecting, and shaping human beings takes a lot of energy. Through God's holy Word and through the power of prayer, may we all grow stronger in the Lord so we can give ourselves to this vital vocation with all the heart and wonder and passion it deserves!

Marian & Anita

The Weight of a Meteor

Reverence for God adds hours to each day.
PROVERBS 10:27 TLB

As a weary mom, you drop into bed with the thundering weight of a meteor hitting the earth. *Wham!* Then your to-do list takes over the sleep you were meant to get. Dishwasher turned on. Check. Kids bathed. Check. Well, sort of. If standing outside in the rain counts. Toys picked up. Check. Well, all the toys are picked up except the ones in the kitchen, living room, and den. And bedrooms. Sigh. . .

The world claims they have all the answers with time-saving technology, time-management seminars, micro-planning, multitasking, and on and on and on. But what God says about getting more done per day isn't always in alignment with what the world preaches.

Proverbs tells us that reverence for God will add hours to our days. What does that look like? Reverence simply means respecting Him. Spending time with Him. Listening to Him. Loving Him. In this sweet, prayerful relationship, He promises to give us more hours in a day. Impossible? Not at all. There may be only twenty-four hours in a day, but there are ways God—the Maker of all time—can order our day so that more is accomplished. More is made satisfying. More can be done with greater meaning and exalted purpose.

The world says, "Hurry up! Do it now!" The world says, "Learn to say no so you can make all your dreams come true." But God says, "Honor me, and I will give you the hours you need for a productive day."

Since the world hasn't gotten it right since the very beginning of time, well, we should go with God.

Lord, please help me honor You in all I do
so that my days can be pleasing and fruitful. Amen.—AH

When Fear Ruins Our Joy

But when he saw the wind, he was afraid and,
beginning to sink, cried out, "Lord, save me!"
MATTHEW 14:30

There is nothing so precious as the sight of a toddler enjoying the world around her. Touching the tickling surface of a gurgling stream. Plucking a bunch of wildflowers just for you. Giggling over the antics of a roly-poly bug. But a mom's joy can turn to panic at the thought of all that can go wrong in her garden of delights. What if her child toddles right into the stream? What if she decides that the flowers are good for tasting as well as looking at? And what if that cute little bug gives her a not-so-cute bite?

What do we do when fear ruins our joy?

Through prayer, let us keep our focus on Christ. When Jesus walked on the water, and Peter had the faith to do the same, he did indeed walk on water. But the moment he looked away from our Lord and concentrated on the roaring sea of all that could go wrong around him, he faltered. He began to sink.

As moms, if we focus on the raging sea—and there will always be some sort of raging sea around us—then we will miss the joy. The small and big daily delights of our children. We will miss the opportunity to influence them. For them to see us walking through this life with confidence in Christ—the same way we hope they will one day walk.

Lord, please help me keep my eyes always on You through
all the calm and stormy seas of motherhood. Amen. —AH

Loved and Refreshed

You make known to me the path of life; you will fill me with joy in your presence, with eternal pleasures at your right hand.
PSALM 16:11

As a mom, sometimes it's wonderful to get away and be with that beloved friend, right? To have a cup of good Italian roast and one of those heart-to-heart chats. Mmmm. Nice. Listening to each other. Telling her about your triumphs and failings and hurts. You'll laugh. You might cry a little. You rejoice. You go away feeling loved and refreshed and a little lighter in spirit.

When we come before God in prayer, it can have many facets, but one of them is fellowship. That is, intimate visits with the one person—Jesus—who longs to spend time with us. Longs to be our beloved friend.

Find a cozy spot, pour a cup of coffee, and get ready for one of those heart-to-heart chats with the Lord. A time for listening to each other. You may be stirred, challenged, redirected, motivated, inspired, changed, and surprised with everlasting delights. You may chuckle a bit. You may be moved to tears of repentance or break out into rejoicing praise. But you will go away feeling loved and refreshed and a little lighter in spirit.

Even as a busy mom, take the time for those heart-to-hearts with the Lord. Take time for the one thing that can make the day clearer, more joyful, and filled with hope and promise. Take time for God.

God, give me a great desire to come before You in humble, heartfelt prayer. I want to have joy in Your presence. Amen. —AH

Those Dumpling Darlings

Jesus often withdrew to lonely places and prayed.
LUKE 5:16

Our children are our dumpling darlings, aren't they? Nothing is too good for them, right? We take great pains to ensure they are encouraged for the days ahead. We watch their sugar intake so they don't swing from the rafters. We monitor their TV time, check their homework, keep an eye on their friends, and encourage a healthy balance in extracurricular activities.

In other words, we can become almost OCD about the intellectual, emotional, and physical well-being of our kids; but how do we handle the most essential part—their spiritual journey? Do they have the light and joy and grace and love of Christ? The peace that surpasses all understanding because they know Christ as the One who loves and redeems them? Do they see us as moms who have a sincere communication with Christ though reading His Word and through prayer? Do they see Christ as a vital part of family life or merely a tradition or cultural obligation?

While on earth, Christ prayed. Even though He was perfect and sinless, His communication with the Father was ongoing and with great fervor. Shouldn't we, as unhappy and misguided folk, have a much greater need to pray for our kids? It's the wisest and most beautiful thing we can do for those dumpling darlings.

Holy Spirit, give me the wisdom and strength I need to point my children toward You. I want to guide them straight into Your loving arms. Amen. —AH

Plenty of Wow Factor

You alone are the Lᴏʀᴅ. You made the heavens, even the highest heavens, and all
their starry host, the earth and all that is on it, the seas and all that is in them.
You give life to everything, and the multitudes of heaven worship you.
Nᴇʜᴇᴍɪᴀʜ 9:6

This verse in Nehemiah is an excellent reminder that God is a glorious Creator. And no one enjoys that creative glory better than a kid. They welcome it. Embrace it. Roll in it.

But as we grow up we seem to misplace some of that curiosity and awareness of the marvelous world around us. In other words, we embrace the mundane rather than the miraculous. Some might even call us a bunch of old cynics! Yes, as the years go by, it takes more and more wow factor to satisfy and surprise us, and yet a child sees serendipities at every turn. They will gasp over the iridescent wings of a butterfly. Or the dewdrops suspended on a spiderweb. Or the confetti rapture of pretty autumn leaves. Or the fuzzy tickle of a caterpillar.

Let us pray that God will renew in us that sense of marvel as well as those sublime imaginings by allowing us to see the world through the eyes of our children. It will not only help us relate to them better, but it will help us worship God in a more reflective and fervent way. Maybe as moms we should encourage our children to pray for us—that the Lord will reawaken in us the marvels and beauty of His good earth.

Creator God, thank You for the exquisite beauty of creation.
Give me fresh eyes so I can be awestruck by You. Amen. —AH

The Apple of His Eye

Neither height nor depth, nor anything else in all creation, will be able to separate us from the love of God that is in Christ Jesus our Lord.
ROMANS 8:39

There are many kinds of prayers. There are the hope-filled ones asking for something we need—or maybe just for something we want. (Hey, that new matching handbag is essential to the overall look!) There are prayers that are shouts of joy, telling God how magnificent He is in all His good works and gifts. There are moments in our prayer time when He draws very near to us, and we whisper our endearments. There are the heart-cries in the middle of the night when we are riddled with doubts and fears.

God has heard prayers on every subject imaginable throughout the ages. So many, in fact, you'd think He would be weary of us all by now. I would be! But the Lord still longs to talk to us. Still longs to help us. Still longs to spend time with us.

Really? You? Me? Why?

Well, don't we just love spending time with our kids? What joy it is. What delight we feel.

You mean God feels that same way about us? Like we're that precious? Even more so? You mean, like we're the apple of His eye?

Yes.

A great big YES!

Father, help me rest in Your abundant love. I am Your beloved child in whom You delight. Allow me to carry that assurance with me wherever I go. Amen. —AH

They Dream Big

I can do all this through him who gives me strength.
PHILIPPIANS 4:13

When kids are little, they naturally believe they can do anything. They are so much fun to watch. They can be aliens, dancers with tour de force moves, ship captains, master chefs of mac and cheese, superheroes. Anything. And nothing seems all that impossible either. They can take an ordinary cardboard box and—with a little paint and tape and crafty genius—create a spaceship that will fly to the moon and back. They dream big. Play hard. Laugh with abandon. And pray and sleep deeply like God really has heard them and He really will watch out for them.

The faith of a child.

Ahh, yes.

In God's Word, Mark touched on this topic, writing, "People were bringing little children to Jesus for him to place his hands on them, but the disciples rebuked them. When Jesus saw this, he was indignant. He said to them, 'Let the little children come to me, and do not hinder them, for the kingdom of God belongs to such as these. Truly I tell you, anyone who will not receive the kingdom of God like a little child will never enter it.' And he took the children in his arms, placed his hands on them and blessed them" (Mark 10:13–16).

Let us pray to find our way back to that kind of simple faith. Our kids will love the way we mother when that kind of prayer is on our lips, in our hearts, and in our lives.

Lord, please cultivate in my heart a radical, childlike faith. Amen. —AH

The Warmth of Heaven

*"For even the Son of Man did not come to be served,
but to serve, and to give his life as a ransom for many."*
MARK 10:45

Motherhood is a fascinating mix of glory and grunt work, but yeah, some days it seems a lot like the latter. With a lot of fixing, scrubbing, hugging, waiting, driving, cooking, serving, cleaning, cleaning, cleaning, cleaning. *Uh-oh.* Got stuck on that last one.

It's easy to find ourselves weary and huddled in the corner swimming in a puddle of tears from all the responsibilities of mom-hood. But in the midst of the triumphs and trials, we can look toward Christ and know that He understands the labors of life. When Jesus came to walk among us, He came as a servant. He came to bring us life eternal. We can't offer that to our children—only Christ can—but He did give us the best example of a life lived with a servant's heart that ever was or ever will be.

Let our daily mom-prayer be to don that kind of Jesus attitude, believing that our toil isn't just work but a great labor of love. Then hopefully, one wonderful day, we will hear our kids say, "Thanks, Mom, for always being there for me. It made all the difference. Oh, and I love you."

That's when we'll smile and our hearts will melt. And we'll feel the warmth of heaven, since God will be smiling, too.

Jesus, thank You for showing me how to be a servant. Give me the
strength and patience to imitate You in every part of my life—
in both the mundane and the marvelous. Amen. —AH

Out of Sheer Joy

*"Here I am! I stand at the door and knock. If anyone hears my voice
and opens the door, I will come in and eat with that person, and they with me."*
REVELATION 3:20

What if you'd prepared a wonderful birthday dinner for your grown son, but he decided that instead of attending the dinner he wanted you to just mail him his birthday gifts. How would that make you feel?

Like dirt.

Sometimes it's easy to treat our Lord the same way. "Sure, I'll take some of those earthly gifts. You know, a singing voice like an angel. A talent for tennis. Good health. A killer wardrobe. A dream house. And any wealth I'm due. Oh, and of course, I want mercy, grace, that gift of salvation, and the eternal life You've offered. Thanks!" Then we forget to show up for the fellowship. The joy. The relationship.

Just as you would welcome your son home to spend some time with you, it's the right thing to do to choose to spend time with our Lord. Not out of obligation. But out of sheer joy.

Yes, Jesus waits for me. He waits for you. It's always a good time to open the door.

Lord, don't let daily distractions and anxieties and to-do lists pull me
away from Your life-giving fellowship. Help me remember that
apart from You, there is no lasting peace or joy. Amen. —AH

Now's the Time

Therefore encourage one another and build
each other up, just as in fact you are doing.
1 THESSALONIANS 5:11

Those little ears. They are so cute. And they are so tuned in to what we say, aren't they? Those little eyes are so beautiful. And they see what we do. More than we know.

How our kids perceive themselves as adults is very much connected to the words and actions they experience growing up. Especially our words and actions. How they see themselves in the mirror is perhaps the way we see them. How they choose their friends may have something to do with the way we choose ours. The way they play, eat, study, work, think, dream—and pray—can be linked to the inner workings of family life.

They may come off as inattentive and oblivious at times, but their hearts are still tender sponges, taking it all in. Even if they don't say so, they long to hear our good words about them just as we long to know God is still in love with us and we're making Him proud. Kids want to hear those same words from us. "You make me proud. I'm so glad you're my child. I enjoy being your mom. I sure do love you."

Have you encouraged your children today? Now's the time. The hour. The moment. . .

Father, help me love my children well—with wisdom, kindness, and patience. May my words encourage them and shape them into the people You want them to be. Amen. —AH

A Little Green Pasture Time

He makes me lie down in green pastures,
he leads me beside quiet waters, he refreshes my soul.
PSALM 23:2–3

What is that horrific hullabaloo? A jackhammer? No. An earthquake? No. It's my child pounding on the bathroom door with a toy dump truck.

Oh happy day.

There doesn't seem to be one moment's peace when you're a full-time mom of wee ones. They are little noise-making machines. They thrive on funky toots and squeals and giggles and chatter and bangs and crashes until you're pulling your already graying hair out by the roots. What to do? Perhaps you could schedule a play day with the neighbor's kids or utilize your church's day care once a week or let the kiddos enjoy some quality time with dear, sweet Grandma.

It may take a bit of arranging, but do take some time off when you can. For fun. For shopping. For lunch out with gal friends. For a stroll at a local park. But most importantly, find those still waters and those green pastures and have some one-on-one time with your Creator God. It will refresh you all the way to your soul. Those hours may seem like a luxury, but really they are a necessity. You'll be a better person. A better wife and friend.

And a better mom.

God, bless me in my efforts to carve out a little extra time for myself—
to be still and bask in Your presence. I can't do this without You. Amen. —AH

The Mega Mommy Meltdown

Above all, love each other deeply, because love covers over a multitude of sins.
1 PETER 4:8

You set out to be the perfect mom. Right?

But that was before your little darling hurled that jar of pureed prunes across the room. Why did she do it? Just to watch it splatter and spurt and spray all over the floor. The curtains. The wallpaper. Your new white shirt. And even the ceiling. Yes, you are headed toward a mega mommy meltdown right there on the kitchen floor.

Being a great mom is a worthy goal, but when we fail, that's when love takes over. It covers a multitude of weaknesses and flaws. If we love our kids deeply and they can see it in our words and actions, they will grow up feeling loved. And that's a good place to be.

How do we love deeply? By staying close to the Lord, reading His Word, and fellowshipping with Him daily. He can teach us how to parent, since He created the very concept and He is the greatest Father of them all!

Messy curtains and wallpaper are the small things in life. Loving our kids deeply? Well, that's the big stuff.

Holy Spirit, when my children try my patience, please remind me of the love You have lavished on me when I've been undeserving and disobedient. I want to love my children deeply, despite their flaws and messy accidents and temper tantrums. Amen. —AH

Love Notes to God

*See what great love the Father has lavished on us, that we
should be called children of God! And that is what we are!*
1 JOHN 3:1

Every day we wake up to God's lavish love. His endearing love notes are all around us. That is, if we choose to take notice. Here's a small list:

A nearby meadow comes to life with the flight of butterflies. An artist gets a burst of creative energy. Our children give us smoochy kisses. A cool breeze refreshes on a hot summer day. The Holy Spirit whispers comfort. God's living Word gives guidance, reproof, and inspiration. There are evergreen boughs hanging heavy with the first winter snow. A friend shares kind or encouraging words. And, of course, there are countless other blessings all around us.

So, what love letters are we giving back to God for His many gifts? Maybe we could bake a casserole for a weary neighbor. We could look up toward the heavens with a bright smile of gratitude. We might sing a praise song before the Lord, letting the Holy Spirit lead us with a new melody and lyrics. We could create something beautiful—like a rose garden—and dedicate it to Him.

Maybe you and your child could come up with some of your own love notes to God. And maybe some of them could come in the form of a bedtime prayer.

Lord, thank You for displaying Your love for me in so many ways.
Don't let me take these love notes for granted. Help me open the eyes of
my children so they can see all the ways You say, "I love you." Amen. —AH

The Big Adventure

"For I know the plans I have for you," declares the L<small>ORD</small>, "plans to prosper
you and not to harm you, plans to give you hope and a future."
JEREMIAH 29:11

Going through life without God's guidance is like driving home with our eyes closed. Things are not going to end well. But thank God, there is a better way to navigate these dangerous streets called life.

And when we consider that divine guidance, we must note that the Almighty created each of us differently. People are like the billions of snowflakes that fall—each are unique and beautiful—none the same. Imagine! Each child has special talents, passions, and his or her own special temperament. With that in mind, what is good for one child may not be good for another. Which is why it may not be wise to insist that our children take on the family business or a profession that is "expected" unless it's God's best for that particular child. Otherwise, our children may miss their big adventure.

So, let's help our children find their calling by praying to the One who designed them. And the One who has a good plan to prosper them, not to harm them, but to give them a hope and a future.

The journey won't necessarily be smooth, but with God's help, there will be joy along the way.

Lord, be a guiding light to my children as they grow and test their wings.
May they look to You during trials and times of decision. Help them
live a life that is pleasing in Your sight. Amen. —AH

Humility Is Mighty

But he gives us more grace. That is why Scripture says:
"God opposes the proud but shows favor to the humble."
JAMES 4:6

$\mathcal{H}$ave you ever been downwind from an industrial-sized pig farm? Believe me, your nostrils will never forget the stinging tang of hog manure. Ever. Have you been downwind from someone who carries the stench of pride? You'll never forget it. Ever You may be chuckling right now. Either because it's kind of funny or because it's kind of true.

Praying for our kids to be humble is great. But God would surely love to see humility in us, too, which would make the life lesson for them more effective. Kids love to emulate us, and they'll pick up on the scent of an arrogant attitude even if we think we have it sufficiently deodorized.

Pride can take many forms. It may be the need to be right. Every. Single. Time. O romancing the notion that we're better than those around us. That we're the squires o our little world—more deserving, more clever, more intelligent, and generally above the common masses.

God opposes this mindset. But He does give grace to those who humble themselves. Humility isn't a cowering spirit, though. Meekness is winsome and wise, but it is never weak. Humility is mighty because it pleases the Lord—and pleasing the Lord is a great spiritual place for our kids—and us—to be.

God, cultivate in me a truly humble spirit.
I want to be an example for my children. Amen. —AH

Then the Angels Celebrated

For God so loved the world that he gave his one and only Son,
that whoever believes in him shall not perish but have eternal life.
JOHN 3:16

This Christian life isn't about self-fulfillment, mindfulness, perfecting oneself, a feel-good theology, or a promise of material wealth. It isn't about working harder and harder to be good enough for heaven.

Christianity is about a beautiful relationship with the One who created us. A relationship for all time with the One who built a bridge to this sin-stained earth so we could be rescued. That bridge has a name. It's Jesus.

When we teach our children to pray, let us not forget to ask them if they are ready to say the most important prayer they will ever pray. The one that says, "Lord Jesus, I believe You are the Son of God. Please forgive me for my sins. Thank You for Your sacrifice on the cross that washes away those sins. I want You to be the Lord of my life, and I want to someday live with You in heaven. Help me live a new life with the power of Your Holy Spirit. In Jesus' name I pray. Amen."

When your children say yes to Christ, don't forget that this is an event worthy of some serious celebrating.

The angels certainly will be.

Holy Spirit, make the gospel new and fresh to me every morning so that my children and others may see its transforming and life-giving power. Amen. —AH

He's Right Here

"Come to me, all you who are weary and burdened, and I will give you rest."
MATTHEW 11:28

The laundry piles are beginning to resemble the peaks of Mount Everest. Your daughter came home with yet another fender bender—her third. It's 98 degrees outside, and the AC guy can't fix the busted air conditioner until next week. Your son's grades plummeted and you have no idea why. The play day you needed for your twins was canceled. And to be honest, you're so tired it's beyond a mere, "I'm bushed, and I need a nap." It's a physical, emotional, spiritual weariness that's become a way of life.

A spa day would help, yes. But the Lord can refresh in a way that is lasting. Meaningful. Profound. Life-changing. So, what does that look like? Feel like?

It's taking time a few minutes before bed to pray and read His Word. Or it's sitting in a quiet place—maybe a prayer closet or porch swing—where you can meet with the One who understands. Who can guide. Who can calm and encourage. Who can be the friend you need. Who can put all earthly trials in perspective. Who can love you no matter what. Who can encourage, challenge, and bring you the peace that passes all understanding. No one else can give that. No one cares like He cares. No one else can bring you to a place of rest and joy like He can.

Jesus is right here. Right now. Always know. . .

Lord, remind me to turn to You for true rest and peace of mind. I need You. Amen. —AH

Beautiful Mystery

*That each of them may eat and drink, and find
satisfaction in all their toil—this is the gift of God.*
ECCLESIASTES 3:13

God wants us to enjoy our lives. Enjoy our children. Enjoy our good work, too! He's given us so many gifts, hasn't He? Including purpose and passion and pleasures.

And the other miraculous detail to this fine story is that He delights in spending time with us as we journey through our days. Just as He enjoyed walking with Adam and Eve in the cool of the day, so He derives joy in walking with us on our many daily paths. He will go along with us as we do our routine chores. As we drive to work, play board games with our children, plant those begonias, and peel those potatoes. As we take that morning jog, offer that cup of cool water to a stranger, sing in the shower, visit an aging relative, discover that breathtaking vista, or let those snowflakes melt on our faces. God is a loving, doting Father.

This facet of God seems too unfathomable—too good to be true. But this is another mystery of His magnificent character, and oh, what a beautiful mystery it is!

Lord, thank You for delighting in me and for desiring a close relationship with me.
Help me grasp the wonder and joy of going through life with You beside me. Amen. —AH

Speaking Truth in Love

"Then you will know the truth, and the truth will set you free."
JOHN 8:32

Truth can be beautiful, and there is a freedom in it, as the scriptures tell us.

But truth can also be permanently wounding when it's offered without love.

God's Word says, "Gracious words are a honeycomb, sweet to the soul and healing to the bones" (Proverbs 16:24).

So, how does one speak the truth when it has the potential to unleash misery? With a heart full of love, there is little room left for an attitude that is power hungry and prideful. One that insists, "I know best, and I'm the perfect person to set you straight!" That mindset won't allow anyone—including our children—to hear the truth.

In addition, in the book of Matthew, we are warned, "You hypocrite, first take the plank out of your own eye, and then you will see clearly to remove the speck from your brother's eye" (Matthew 7:5).

What is the answer then? Let us ask the Holy Spirit to guide us in our words. That as we speak the truth, we have discernment, courage, wisdom, humility, and a gracious spirit. Let it be said that we are not just mothers who are full of truth but full of love.

God, give me boldness to speak the truth but also a gentle tongue softened by love. Make me aware of my own sin so that I can remain humble. Amen. —AH

Those Adorable Little Rascals

I praise you because I am fearfully and wonderfully made;
your works are wonderful, I know that full well.

PSALM 139:14

*S*chool's out for summer vacation. Yay!

Well, sort of yay.

You're driving them home from school on that last day, and your son starts to give enough love-pokes to his sister to get her wailing, "Mom, make him stop." Now your daughter retaliates by throwing his favorite action hero out the window. Your son bellows, "Look what she did!" Then, of course, you know it's going to be all-out war for the whole looong summer. And somewhere in all of that hurly-burly mess, you start to think of your adorable little rascals as not-so-adorable little monsters.

It's easy to get lost in the minutiae of motherhood. That is, focusing on those peevish moments rather than the miracles.

And each child is that—a genuine miracle—just as you are. We are to praise God, knowing we are wonderfully made. None of us alike. None of us mundane. But instead, handmade in His image.

So, on those trying days of motherhood—when you want to pull out those newly graying hairs—remember that your child has a beautiful destiny. With a prayerful heart toward God, you'll have the privilege and pleasure to help him or her find out just what that calling is.

Father, give me strength and patience during those long summer days when rest or a quiet moment seem impossible. Help me see my children through Your eyes. Amen. —AH

Learning to Pray

Therefore confess your sins to each other and pray for each other so that you may be healed. The prayer of a righteous person is powerful and effective.
JAMES 5:16

No matter how healthy you are as a mom, you're bound to get sick on occasion, but motherhood just keeps rolling on.

What to do? You could ask your kids for help. Of course, that could get complicated when they take over the chores without supervision. For instance, after they've brought you your breakfast-in-bed, they may mention that the jam-slathered toast you just ate had first made a landing on the kitchen floor—facedown. Or when they've helped with the laundry, your cell phone got a good washing along with your jeans. Or your personal favorite: You've awakened to a finger painting of a rainbow on your bedroom wall—the one meant to make Mommy feel better. *Sigh.*

On second thought, you could have your husband take a day of vacation. Or use the superb services of grandparents or enlist the help of a trusted neighbor or friend. But when your kids gather around your bed wanting to help Mom in some way, you could say, "You know what? Mom is the one sick this time, and I need your prayers. Will you kneel down beside me and ask God to heal me?"

God wants us to pray for each other, and so what a great time for our kids to learn that we value their prayers and that God does, too.

Lord, thank You for hearing and honoring our prayers. Thank You for stooping down to listen to the whispered prayers of meek children. Amen. —AH

Those Tender Shoots

May these words of my mouth and this meditation of my heart
be pleasing in your sight, LORD, my Rock and my Redeemer.
PSALM 19:14

When going on woodland walks in state parks, sometimes hikers will see a sign warning them not to veer from the trail so they don't step on the delicate vegetation. The rangers are just being careful to preserve the landscape for future guests.

Hopefully when it comes to our kids, we are even more careful with our words, so we don't trample their tender spirits. Obviously, our children are far more precious than ferns and moss, and yet in a fit of anger, it's easy to say things that we'll regret later. Words that could crush them and cause them emotional damage that could last a lifetime.

In the book of Psalms, we are encouraged to please the Lord with our thoughts and words. When we make it a priority to meet this criterion, we are bound to get it right. . .when it comes to what we say as we're disciplining our kids, when we're angry with them, or when we're just bone tired.

Psalm 19:14 would make a great prayer for every morning. In fact, it would make a good life-prayer for all moms.

Lord, I want my words to be pleasing in Your sight. When I'm frustrated and angry, help me bridle my tongue and say only things that are constructive and kind. May my words be tools that help support and build up my children. Amen. —AH

The Sharp Teeth of Worry

Do not be anxious about anything, but in every situation,
by prayer and petition, with thanksgiving, present your requests to God.
PHILIPPIANS 4:6

When we slip into bed, sometimes worries come nibbling at us like little fishies on our toes. But sometimes those fishies have very sharp teeth, and it might take hours to get to sleep. Then we wake up unsettled as the cares of the days weigh in. Or maybe we wake up early to get a head start on our fretting. Hey, somebody has to do the job, right?

As a mom, no matter what stage of life our children are in, there are plenty of things to keep us anxious at all hours of the day and night. And yet, the Bible tells us not to live that way. Not to fret, but to come to Him with everything worrisome. Big things. Little stuff. And everything in between.

Coming to the Lord in prayer with a heart of thanksgiving helps. Love and a grateful spirit will crowd out the fear, since we are also told in 1 John 4:18 that "there is no fear in love. But perfect love drives out fear, because fear has to do with punishment. The one who fears is not made perfect in love."

If our hands are still in wringing-fist mode, we may need to give our troubles to Jesus again. He won't be angry. He'll be glad we've come, and He'll help us unloose our fingers one by one so we can lift them toward the heavens. To worship. To praise. To finally rest without fear.

Jesus, I surrender my concerns, anxieties, and frustrations to You.
Don't let me hold back. You are in control. Amen. —AH

Serious Hope

For our struggle is not against flesh and blood, but against the rulers,
against the authorities, against the powers of this dark world and
against the spiritual forces of evil in the heavenly realms.
EPHESIANS 6:12

If we ever for one minute think we're safe, then we are merely fooling ourselves. This life is riddled with peril from the moment we take our first gasping breath to the very last sigh. Not just dangerous for us but for each member of our family. For our parents. Our friends. Our coworkers. Our children. This is not paradise any longer. We gave up that right when sin came into the world through disobedience. This world is seriously out of control.

So, what can anyone do if getting up in the morning is such a risky endeavor?

Pray hard. Pray about everything. And have faith that He is listening. That He will be by your side no matter what. It is the only way to navigate through this spiritual battlefield. Because as it says in Ephesians, we are fighting against the spiritual forces of evil in the heavenly realms. If you don't believe it, turn on the news. It's everywhere. Impossible to miss. But there is always an answer—one answer:

Jesus.

So, pray a prayer of protection over your children. Pray and believe that God has their best interest at heart, forever working all things for good. In a perilous world, these words carry serious help and serious hope for mothers.

Father, please bless and protect my family in this risky life.
Help me trust in Your sovereign plan for our lives. Amen. —AH

That Thing We Do

Whatever you do, work at it with all your heart,
as working for the Lord, not for human masters.
COLOSSIANS 3:23

*M*othering. It's an amazing occupation. It requires strength, inspiration, love, courage, patience, patience. Patience. Did I say patience? And on some days, it may seem like what we are trying to accomplish is nearly impossible.

But there's good news. The Lord loves our line of work—it is a gift from Him, in fact—and He is cheering us on. We don't have to live with the stress of thinking we are striving to please people. If we ask the Lord, He will be our supervisor, and He will guide us with a gentle and steady hand. He is, after all, the greatest of all parents. So, as we work in this beautiful profession, we are toiling alongside Him, gaining wisdom and knowledge each step of the way.

Let us pray we do this mothering mission with all our hearts. With great joy. That heart-delight will show in our countenance, and it will show as our children grow up and enter the world. All that joy and love and light of Christ will not only flow into our kids, but it will flow out of them into a lost and troubled world.

Yes, we work for the Lord, and it is good!

God, give me overflowing joy in all my endeavors, both great and small.
I want the light of Your Spirit to shine through my words and actions. Amen. —AH

Singing over Our Kids

"The LORD your God is with you, the Mighty Warrior who saves.
He will take great delight in you; in his love he will no
longer rebuke you, but will rejoice over you with singing."
ZEPHANIAH 3:17

The mood in a room can change in an instant with the right music. Have you ever noticed that? There is something about the magic of a melody that has the power to soothe us, revive us, make us feel loved, or create any number of emotions.

In the book of Zephaniah, we are told that God rejoices over us and even sings. What would that kind of divine song sound like? A lullaby? A stirring song as one who wins a spiritual battle? Maybe God has a special song for each and every person born. One that calls us to Him like a love song. Why not, since He is the great lover of our souls? Whatever kind of song it is, we can be assured that God's music would be much more exquisite than anything we've ever heard on earth. It would be far beyond all our imaginings.

If singing over your kids isn't really your thing—or you consider your crooning to be more of a yowl than melodious—maybe you could prayerfully find ways to let them know how much you delight in them and the many ways they've added to the beautiful harmony of your family. Even if there isn't a song on your lips, they'll enjoy the one playing in your heart.

Mighty God, how wonderful that You rejoice and sing over us—Your children.
Because of Your loving example, I can better cherish my own children. Amen. —AH

Will You Forgive Me?

Be kind and compassionate to one another,
forgiving each other, just as in Christ God forgave you.
EPHESIANS 4:32

Okay, so your child accidentally put gum in your hair while you were taking a nap. Or maybe it wasn't so much an accident as an experiment. You know, just to see how sticky gum really is. Later, your little darling let the dog out and your newly planted petunias got trampled. Your daughter took the keys to the car without permission. Your son slammed the bedroom door, but before he did, he said some things that he shouldn't have said. In fact, truth be known, you both said things that were unkind and maybe even a bit cruel.

Thank God for forgiveness. It's one word that has the power to change everything.

We might think, "The wound is deep. I'm not sure I can forgive." But if we make a list of the offenses we've made against God and man through the years, we may be working on that list for quite a while. God forgave us for all our sins, and He expects us to forgive others, including our kids. As we forgive others, sometimes those four words will need to come from us, "Will you forgive me?"

Let us pray for a humble attitude so we can forgive as well as ask for forgiveness. It's freeing. It's healing. It will change everything.

Lord, help me place past hurts in Your hands. Give me the strength to let go of bitterness and pride and to instead embrace the freedom of forgiveness—in both giving and receiving. Amen. —AH

Speaking Truth

Instead, speaking the truth in love, we will grow to become in every respect the mature body of him who is the head, that is, Christ.
EPHESIANS 4:15

Speaking truth in love sounds easy at first. Praise rolls off most mothers' tongues like dew off of honeysuckle blossoms. "You're so big!" "Great job, buddy!"

But those babies grow and listen to other voices, mimicking their words or even their thinking. It's all fine and dandy as long as we like the people they are imitating. If we don't. . .conflict begins. But that's where growing up starts, too—for both mother and child.

Praise is naturally delivered in a package of love. Words of support and encouragement are nourishing bits of sweetness to anyone's soul. But Paul was talking to the Ephesians about other words. These are the hard words you have to compose when people you love have been deceived or are deceiving themselves (like those infants, tossed back and forth or blown here and there, in verse 14). These are messages that say, "No," "Stop," "Don't," "Wait."

For these messages to be effective, they have to be prayerfully considered and carefully wrapped. They have to come from someone who really knows the hearer. They have to come from someone who really cares about what's best for the other person. And they have to come from someone who's willing to stick around long enough to see the results.

Sounds like a job just right for a mother.

Dear Lord, help me to choose my words well and to speak Your truth in love (and not just my own opinion in haste). Amen. —ML

Let Time Stand Still

So the sun stood still, and the moon stopped,
till the nation avenged itself on its enemies.
JOSHUA 10:13

How many times have you asked God to make time stop? How often have you wished your children would not grow up quite so quickly? (Or at least not skip three sizes of clothing in one summer!)

Joshua did not make the sun stand still to slow his children's growth. But then, Joshua didn't make the sun stand still at all. It was God.

God helped Joshua take down Jericho and Ai. And when five kings joined forces against the Gibeonites, and the Gibeonites asked Joshua for help, it was God who told Joshua not to be afraid: "I have given them into your hand. Not one of them will be able to withstand you" (Joshua 10:8).

So Joshua marched confidently against those five armies and right into the win God had already claimed. Joshua 10:14 says, "There has never been a day like it before or since."

This story reminds us that God has already given us all we need. We don't need to worry about the coming days, the coming battles. We don't even have to worry about our children growing too fast. And we definitely shouldn't waste a moment of now fretting about the days that were or the days that will be. The God who put the sun into the sky and can freeze it there has already claimed victory over our great enemy. And He holds us in His hand.

Lord, thank You for listening to me and freezing my fears. Amen. —ML

Acts of Compassion

Jesus wept.
JOHN 11:35

"Lord, the one you love is sick" (John 11:3). That was the message that came to Jesus. Those seven little words tell us much. Jesus had a special relationship with this family. It was special enough that He was willing to risk a stoning to visit with these grieving friends.

When Jesus arrived at the home in Bethany, first Martha then Mary came out to meet Him. Mary fell at His feet. As the beginning of the chapter points out, this wasn't the first time Mary had fallen at Jesus' feet. It wasn't the first time she came to Him grieving what she had lost.

Jesus saw this woman's tears. He saw the others gathered there weeping. And He, being both fully human and purely humane, wept, too. He was "deeply moved in spirit and troubled" (verse 33).

He came to them. He listened to them. He cried with them. He did all the things we should do for those who are hurting and for those, like our children, who need to see an example of active compassion.

But Jesus, being also fully God, did not stop there. He didn't just give a little to His friends. He gave everything He had. And that power was enough to raise a man from the dead.

We don't have the same power as Jesus. But we can have that kind of compassion. It's the kind that takes risks to care for others. Compassion that reaches out even when it's hard. Compassion that hurts when others hurt.

Lord, help me to hurt when others hurt. And help me
to take action to make a difference. Amen. —ML

Enough

"Your servant has nothing there at all," she said, "except a small jar of olive oil."
2 KINGS 4:2

The poor widow was desperate. There was nothing left. Every crumb had been eaten. Every stitch had been sold. Every favor used up. If she had any friends left, they had nothing to offer. She had nothing with which to trade. Nothing to make promises on. No skill that was worth enough. No time left. Nothing at all, except a few spoons of olive oil.

Have you been there—feeling like you have nothing left to give? And yet, children are still hungry and waiting and coming to you for answers. Can you stretch yourself enough to be there for them? To make answers appear?

All God wants from you are empty jars.

Elisha said to this mother of two boys, "Go around and ask your neighbors for empty jars. Don't ask for just a few " (2 Kings 4:3).

It's fun to think of her gathering the jars from her sons' arms, closing the door, and pouring the oil, just as Elisha instructed. Just imagine the moment when she realized all would be well. Was it the first jar? Or was it the sixth? At what point did she stop counting the drops and start realizing that she could count on God? God knew exactly what she needed. And He would provide that, and so much more.

Next time you wonder if you are enough, open your hands and give God your emptiness. Depend on Him. Then get ready to receive His blessings.

Don't ask for just a few.

Lord of plenty, help me trust You when I am empty. Amen. —ML

With a Flourish

May the LORD cause you to flourish, both you and your children.
May you be blessed by the LORD, the Maker of heaven and earth.
PSALM 115:14–15

There are many words we don't use nearly often enough anymore. *Flourish* is one of those. Perhaps it's because not enough of us are doing it.

To flourish is the opposite of just getting by, surviving, making ends meet. To flourish means you have everything you need to not only come out all right but to prosper. To be successful. To be beautiful.

At the base of the word *flourish* is a root that comes from Latin, meaning "flower." A flourishing yard is not one that has grass that isn't brown and is kept marginally tidy. A flourishing yard is one that is so healthy, it announces it in vibrant, living color— lush green grass, full flower beds, strong trees.

But no yard gets that way by just watching the grass grow. It takes hard work. It takes wisdom. It takes thoughtfulness. It takes good seeds planted in fertile soil.

It will certainly take the hand of God. Thankfully, He's already provided us a way to have access to His expertise. All we have to do is. . .ask.

Lord, please cause us to grow into what You want us to be. Please help us provide a healthy environment for our children that will allow them to grow, too. Amen. —ML

Darkness into Light

You, Lord, are my lamp; the Lord turns my darkness into light.
2 SAMUEL 22:29

"Mommy?" the little voice calls from behind the bedroom door. "Could you leave a light on, please?"

Many mothers hear this call each night. It's become part of the routine. It is natural for children to fear the darkness. We all get a bit on edge when we can't see where we're headed—or who might be in our path.

How wonderful it is to know that God not only brings light to the darkness—He actually can change the darkness! He can because He is in the darkness and formed the darkness. He knows every corner of the night. He knows every shadow's name.

Genesis 1 tells us that the Spirit of God was there, hovering over the deep waters, before light was even called. Exodus tells us that Moses "approached the thick darkness where God was" (Exodus 20:21). Job says that God "reveals the deep things of darkness" (Job 12:22). In David's song of praise to God, he says that our Lord "made darkness his canopy around him" (2 Samuel 22:12).

If your child is struggling against the phantoms of the night—or you are—take heart in knowing that our God is in control. The night will keep coming, but God can take the dark, fearful thoughts within us and reshape them into wisdom, into thoughtfulness, into light.

But it's still okay to leave a light on.

God, who made the light and darkness, please help
me control my fearful thoughts. Amen. —ML

Of Seeds and Mountains

"Because you have so little faith. Truly I tell you, if you have faith as small as a mustard seed, you can say to this mountain, 'Move from here to there,' and it will move. Nothing will be impossible for you."
MATTHEW 17:20

Impossible. How many times have you had that thought when faced with a monumental task—a mountain of post-campout laundry, the not-yet-started historical diorama that your kiddo has due tomorrow, the children who have taken sibling rivalry to new levels?

Ridiculous. Some things seem so far out of your realm that the idea of even attempting to manage them is laughable. Except no one is laughing.

Perhaps you have never ordered your laundry basket to move, but maybe you've faced other kinds of mountains in your life. Maybe you're staring up a steep grade right now. It's good to know a little faith will go a long way.

The tiny, round mustard seed is nothing much to look at. It's easily lost (especially if you don't have the lid on the spice bottle tight and it spills out onto the slippery kitchen floor). But that little seed has everything in it to grow into a mustard plant—something that can produce more seeds, which can produce more plants or spices to season all kinds of foods.

A little bit of faith may not look like much. It may not be something you post about on Facebook. But in a little seed of faith is everything you need to grow and do the things God has set before you to do—even five loads of mud-soaked laundry.

Lord, help me keep believing in You. Amen. —ML

Sparks

Consider what a great forest is set on fire by a small spark.
JAMES 3:5

Sometimes it starts with just a smirk in response. An eye roll that's a little too obvious. A noise of disapproval. A grunt of disgust you didn't quite keep your kid from hearing. A sigh of discontent.

It doesn't take much. One hint of implication. One line written in haste. One picture that only shows a part of the story. It doesn't take much to hurt your child's trust.

In this day and age when we have more and faster forms of communication than ever before, it's surprisingly easy to both receive and spread misinformation. Making assumptions, jumping to conclusions, and sitting in judgment have become favorite hobbies. And sadly, moms are often the ones taking on these hobbies.

It's just too easy.

It's also easy to think it doesn't matter that much. But it does. Before you repeat a story, put words in someone's mouth, or make a complaint—especially when it's about someone in your own family—consider that big forest James talked about. Think of the last time you watched a fire burn. Just the tiniest of sparks is all that's necessary to make the wood crackle and curl. Thick, heavy logs crumble to dust in minutes. Trunks that supported shade-giving branches and the homes of small creatures can disintegrate into a pile of gray ashes.

It's just too easy.

But then again, is it really that hard to hold your tongue? To press pause? To wait to hear the whole story? To ask God for discernment?

Lord, help me keep my lips zipped and my eyes on You. Amen. —ML

Peace Child

The wolf will live with the lamb, the leopard will lie down with the goat,
the calf and the lion and the yearling together; and a little child will lead them.
ISAIAH 11:6

There's something about small children that just brings people together. Even before they make it out of the womb, the announcement of pending births can make people smile and gather in celebration. The sight of a pregnant belly causes perfect strangers to suddenly forget all personal boundaries—with curious fingers, they reach out to touch the place where life is growing.

Old wounds heal, rifts are mended, arguments are forgotten when a baby arrives on the scene. It's as if, perhaps, in that moment when we see the tiny toes curl and smell the sweet tops of their heads, we suddenly remember that this is what we all were once. We were all new and clean, unscarred and unbroken. We were all helpless and needy, hungry and small.

Perhaps God sent Jesus as a baby for this very reason. To remind us that we were all once children. That we all need to be fed and cared for. And that sometimes everyone just needs to be held a little tighter.

Lord, help us let little children lead us in knowing and enjoying and living in the peace that only comes through You. Help us share that peace with all who cross our paths, even our enemies. Amen. —ML

Light on the Pepper

Let your conversation be always full of grace, seasoned with salt,
so that you may know how to answer everyone.
COLOSSIANS 4:6

$\mathcal{S}$alt is a preservative. Before the days of Maytag, foods were kept in an edible state for longer periods of time by adding salt. For thousands of years, this valuable seasoning was used as a form of currency—an item that could be traded for precious goods.

The words we use in our conversations should be words that will preserve the most nourishing parts of our relationships. They should be words that soothe or comfort, words that make us laugh at ourselves, and even words that add a little spice—perhaps that spark a good debate or cause us to ask interesting questions.

Valuable messages require more care than others. Paul warned the Colossians to be wise in the way they acted toward outsiders. He wanted them to use any opportunity to spread the message of the Gospel. To do that, they'd have to bring the outsiders in and they'd have to be careful not only in what words they chose, but in how they spoke them.

A message of "I love you" is hard to take if it's spat at you—even if it comes from your own mother. And if a person doesn't think you care at all about them, why should they care what you have to say? If your children don't think you care that much about their problems, why should they care what you have to say about their souls?

Lord, help my words be patient and forgiving, caring and careful,
especially when I speak with anyone about the gospel. Amen. —ML

Fine Speeches

"I also could speak like you, if you were in my place;
I could make fine speeches against you and shake my head at you."
JOB 16:4

Job had had enough. He was in the middle of the worst suffering anyone's ever written about, and his friends were being about as comforting as a wet blanket during a chilly Saturday morning soccer game. In one of the many cycles of lament and accusation in this poetic book, the hero of our story spits back a reply at his "miserable comforters."

Now we often hear Job's patience praised—but it seems from passages like this one that he wasn't all that patient really. Job was persistent. He endured. He kept going, even when the going got hard, and harder, and absolutely the hardest. But he didn't always go with grace. There was a good deal of bitterness in his words.

However, he was honest. And in these exchanges with his so-called friends, where the bitterness and anger and sorrow flushes out, we might just want to pause a moment, look at the picture, and wonder, *What would I have said?*

What do you say? When someone's having a horrible time and you arrive on the scene—are you comforting? Or are you critical? What about when the someone is a certain young friend of yours—or your own wandering teenager? Do you make fine speeches that sting instead of soothe? Do you offer glum predictions instead of grace? When correction is warranted, is it spoken in love and truth or just spewed out with a generous helping of "I told you so" on top?

Lord, help me guard my tongue against making fine speeches that could hurt instead of help. Amen. —ML

Few

God is in heaven and you are on earth, so let your words be few.
ECCLESIASTES 5:2

God, You are big, and I am small.
    You are forever, and I am fleeting.
    You are mighty, and I only wish I might.
    You are a rock, and I am sand.
    You are the wind, and I am blown.
    You are music, and I am noise.
    You are light, and I am a shadow.
    You are wisdom, and I know so little.
    You are a story, and I am a sentence.
    You are the beginning and end, and I am a moment in the middle.
    You are strong coffee, and I am weak tea.
    You are a burning fire, and I am an ash.
    You are the director, and I say my lines.
    You are the artist, and I am a bit of blank space.
    You are the counselor, and I call out to You.
    You are the maker, and I am made.
    You are the whole, and I am a part.
    You are the One Father, and I'm just one mom.
    You are the caller of children, and I am Your child.

Lord, thank You for listening. Help me always remember how big You are. Amen. —ML

Drink

*Like a snow-cooled drink at harvest time is a trustworthy messenger
to the one who sends him; he refreshes the spirit of his master.*
PROVERBS 25:13

You can taste the sweat. One drop rolls down the curve of your forehead, along your nose, into the valley above your lip. It's warm and salty as it touches your tongue. It tastes of work and summer and days that seem to never end.

But it is not refreshing.

It doesn't really matter whether on a farm or in a factory or in the delivery room—it's likely that every one of us has had at least one hard job in our lives. A task that pushed us beyond what we thought we could bear. Labor that seemed too hot, too long, too difficult.

The prayers prayed in moments like these often come in grunts. A mere exhale of energy and a gasp for hope. Our lips are too dry to form words, and our minds cannot grasp meaning in the fog of exhaustion.

But we can still pray. Our hearts reach out to God. He knows what we want. He supplies what we need. And the feeling of peace that comes when He whispers to us is better than any drink. We can read His Word, and the messages there cool our thoughts. We rest in a moment of stillness with Him, and our heartbeats start to slow down.

The trustworthy messenger refreshes his master, but the message our God sends us brings new life to all who hear it. Sometimes it brings new life right into our laps.

Drink His words in today.

God, You are a great communicator. Help me carry
Your refreshing Word to others today. Amen. —ML

Giving in Grace

But since you excel in everything—in faith, in speech, in knowledge,
in complete earnestness and in the love we have kindled in you—
see that you also excel in this grace of giving.
2 CORINTHIANS 8:7

This congregation would have been the pride of any pastor. They were grounded firmly in their beliefs. They had control of their tongues and used words wisely. They had listened well to the messages Paul and others had brought to them. And they loved each other and the followers of Christ who helped teach them about His story. They were excelling in many ways, but there was one more thing Paul just had to bring up—giving.

Budgeting is hard. Making money stretch to meet all that kids need these days is not fun. And then giving more on top of all that? Sometimes it just doesn't seem possible.

But Paul wanted to wake these Corinthians up. He wanted to stretch them. And God wants to stretch us, too. Listen to more of Paul's message for the church at Corinth (verse 9): "For you know the grace of our Lord Jesus Christ, that though he was rich, yet for your sake he became poor, so that you through his poverty might become rich."

You know that grace. The grace that does the impossible. The grace that gives more than is necessary. The grace that counts the cost but then forgets the debt.

This is the grace that Paul wanted the Corinthians to excel in. And it's the grace we need to live in. And the grace we need to show our kids.

God, please help me be willing to give everything for You. Amen. —ML

Surprise

He settles the childless woman in her home as
a happy mother of children. Praise the Lord.
PSALM 113:9

God surprises us. He surprises us in the same way we are taken aback by a distinctly beautiful sunrise or by the vivid ribbons of sunset on the ocean.

If we could somehow hold His greatness in our minds every moment, perhaps these acts would not be so surprising. Maybe then we would not worry. When day after day is dull and gray, when the sun never seems to shine, when all we feel is loss and all we hold slips away—on these days, if we could just remember who He is, we could put our anxieties to rest.

How many times do you stop to think about who our God is? Who is like Him? He is the God of contradictions. He is the God of plot twists. He is the God of surprise endings.

He is seated on the best throne, a seat in the highest heavens. Yet He—Creator of the universe—stoops down to look on us, to care for us.

He can lift the poor and needy out of the dust—not just to make them clean, but to make them like princes.

And He can take a woman who has longed for children—a woman who has heard the words "statistically unlikely" one too many times, whose arms ache for the weight of a baby—and settle her in her own home, with her children nestled around her.

Lord, thank You for the blessing of children. And thank You for surprising us. Amen. —ML

Actions Do Speak Loudly

Dear children, let us not love with words or speech but with actions and in truth.
1 JOHN 3:18

Spelling words on the go; hair braided just so.
Lunch money remembered then forgot, but Mom brings it to school on the spot.
Birthday cakes in the latest style; holes sewn up to last another mile.
Hands that wrestle fitted sheets and tuck in blankets around our feet.
Little notes written just for a day away; sharp words remind us not to stray.
Calendars filled with times and dates—activities to suit every trait.
Gifts thought about, planned, worked for, and bought—then taken back without a word if the size is a bit off.
Carpool madness, trophies won; staying up to "help" till a quarter past one.
Cleaned-up messes, cooked-up treats; shelves stocked with all our favorite eats. . . .

Most moms and dads have the "with actions" part of love down.

But sometimes, when that new pair of jeans comes home with a hole or the homework book gets left at school for the seventh time in a week, suddenly the words and speech become a big problem. Criticism and complaint fairly leap out of our mouths.

It's just at those times, though, when the actions mean more than ever. Because the children who are getting a scolding will know, deep down, that the person yelling at them now is also the person who stayed up late doing laundry and got up early to get them to practice on time.

And that person may be pretty mad right now, but she for sure loves them.

She just needs a nap!

Lord, help me love my children with actions and in truth. Amen. —ML

Downy Refuge

How priceless is your unfailing love, O God!
People take refuge in the shadow of your wings.
PSALM 36:7

Let's be honest for a second. Most baby birds are downright ugly when they're very young. Tiny balls of bones and fluff—they can barely hold their heavy heads up at first.

They need warmth. Their downy layer is not fully formed. In fact, they look about half-plucked. They are easy targets for all kinds of prey. Even when they do get a bit more photogenic and fluffy, they're not out of harm's way. Without their outer feathers, designed to protect against the elements, baby birds are easily soaked to the skin and reduced to cold, shivering, laundry lint lumps.

But when the rains come, the little ones don't have to be afraid. They just stay close to their mama, and she takes care of the rest. She gathers her babies under her big, water-repellent wings and she cranks up her body heat. The little ducklings get a front-row seat on their very own heated tour bus.

God designed mothers well. He equipped them with the physical ability to shield and protect, along with the mental desire to care for others. And he sealed all of that up with a heart full of love for our babies.

When we see a mother with her chicks, we can remember two things: Thank God for designing His creatures so carefully, but also know that, when the rains come, we don't have to be afraid. All we have to do is stay close to Him, and He will take care of the rest.

Lord, thank You for Your unfailing love. Please be my refuge. Amen. —ML

Examples

Don't let anyone look down on you because you are young, but set an example
for the believers in speech, in conduct, in love, in faith and in purity.
1 TIMOTHY 4:12

These words go out to all the young mothers or the new mothers out there in the world—no matter your age.

Don't let other people bother you. Don't pay too much attention to unsolicited advice and unwanted tips. Don't worry overmuch about the proper way to do a thing or the wisdom of a thousand experts. Don't doubt your instincts and your heart.

Consider this for a moment: everyone (and their mother) has an opinion about raising kids. They can't all be right! But God's wisdom can help in any situation.

Set an example for other young mothers by being careful with your words. Don't be overly boastful or complain too frequently. Be humble and gracious in your interactions with others. Be grateful for what people give you—and be discreet in what you return.

Get comfortable with love in all its forms. Realize that love is in cleaning up spit-up at 2:00 a.m. just as much as it is in snuggles against freshly washed baby skin.

In the middle of all the mess and miracles, remember your Maker. Read His Word, talk to Him every day, and don't give up on church. Keep reaching out to your church family—treat them like the brothers and sisters that they are.

Keep your mind and heart focused on Him, and keep your chin up! As you grow stronger in your faith, you'll be stronger for your baby, too.

Lord, bring us all good examples of motherhood.
Help us build each other up. Amen. —ML

Prayer Simplified

"Your kingdom come, your will be done."
MATTHEW 6:10

∾

*R*ight in the middle of His Sermon on the Mount, Jesus talks to the crowds about three very routine faith practices: giving to the needy, prayer, and fasting. The common message in all three is—don't practice your faith as a show. Your faith is not for others—it's for you and God.

Sticking to the Christian life is not always the easiest thing to do. Jesus tries to break it down for us in simple, clear steps. But even then we may miss it. It's good to look back at His instructions and commit to keep trying and also to teach our children in the same way.

In what we all know as the Lord's Prayer, Jesus tells us to do these things when we pray: recognize who God is, ask Him to show His will, ask for His provision, recognize our own need to be forgiven and to forgive, and be honest about our weaknesses.

At the core of Jesus' teaching on that mountainside are these words, located in the heart of the Lord's Prayer: "Your kingdom come, your will be done." So much can be achieved by simply praying that prayer every morning: God, remind me how I'm living in Your kingdom and show me Your will for me in it today.

Let's all pray that prayer together today.

Our Father—let Your kingdom come and Your will be done today. Amen. —ML

Mother of Nations

"I will bless her so that she will be the mother of nations;
kings of peoples will come from her."
GENESIS 17:16

*E*ver wonder what ninety-year-old Sarah felt when she heard she was going to be the "mother of nations"?

Overwhelmed?

Nervous?

Just plain tired?

In Genesis 18 we read about the famous meeting of Abraham and three visitors, and it is then Sarah actually laughs at the promise of her giving birth in a year's time. Artists often depict this scene with Sarah laughing joyously, as if she's just received some lovely news. But most older women who find out all of a sudden that they are pregnant will take in that news with a mixture of surprise, gladness, and a healthy dose of fear.

For Sarah, this news must have carried with it some extra nerve-racking possibilities. For after all, though just one baby was discussed then, that phrase "mother of nations" was hanging out there. Exactly how many children was she supposed to carry? How many babies would she labor with and deliver? How many trips to the hospital was this supposed to take?

As usual, God had it all under control. Sarah may have missed His signal, but it's there in Genesis 17:16: "I will bless her so that." God would not leave Sarah on her own. He was going to equip her to take her place as mother of nations—He would supply her with all the diapers and wipes she needed. Okay, maybe not—but you get the idea.

And you know what? He'll equip you with what you need, too.

Lord, thank You for supplying us with what we need so
we can do amazing things with You. Amen. —ML

Better Than Seven Sons

"For your daughter-in-law, who loves you and who is better to you than seven sons, has given him birth."

RUTH 4:15

Some people say there's nothing better than becoming a mother—except becoming a grandmother. For Naomi, this joy must have been especially sweet.

After losing her husband and her own two sons to illness, Naomi was in mourning. She just wanted to go to her homeland and be alone. She was bitter and sad. She didn't understand why God had done this to her—for in her thinking, that was what had happened. God had purposely inflicted suffering upon her.

Her words to the women of Bethlehem reflect her feelings quite plainly: "I went away full, but the LORD has brought me back empty" (Ruth 1:21).

Of course, what Naomi wasn't counting in her assessment was her daughter-in-law—Ruth, the woman who had begged to stay with her, until death parted them.

As Naomi's story unfolds, we see just how valuable Ruth became to Naomi, and we see Naomi understanding that perhaps things were not all that they had seemed through her eyes of suffering.

Who is valuable to you in your life? Whom might you be overlooking? Who is wanting to be a bigger part of your family? Take a look around. God may have blessings for you that you haven't even considered yet.

Naomi's story ends with the women of Bethlehem—who had before been shocked at the sight of sorrowful Naomi—rejoicing with Naomi over her growing family. And Grandma Naomi takes the boy into her no longer empty arms.

Lord, show me the people in my life I may be overlooking.
Teach me to be grateful for my blessings. Amen. —ML

Glimpses of Sorrow

"I have been praying here out of my great anguish and grief."
1 SAMUEL 1:16

Oh Hannah!

Here is a picture of a woman grieving the loss of children she could not have. Year after long year, she weeps and suffers. She can't eat. To make it all worse, she is forever being reminded of her lack by her rival. And her husband doesn't understand her pain. He loves her and wants her to be happy—to be at peace (and probably to stop crying so much). But he can't supply what she needs.

So she goes to the only one who will understand. The only one who knows suffering better than anyone. And she is not disappointed.

But this is not just a story of a woman crying out to God and God supplying her with a child. It's a story that tells us something about grief and how to help those who grieve among us.

First, even in her grief, Hannah kept worshipping the Lord. She stayed faithful to Him, and He was faithful to her.

Second, nowhere in this story do we see any evidence that God thought her grieving was wrong. Instead, God "remembered her" in her grief. It's okay to be sad.

Lastly, people who are close to a grieving person often get it wrong. Hannah's husband tried to be helpful, but he didn't understand how. The priest jumped to the wrong conclusion about her. We need to be patient and try to hear someone's story before we attempt to give any answers.

God of many sorrows, help us understand and
help those who are grieving today. Amen. —ML

Not Yet Known

Dear friends, now we are children of God, and what we will be has not yet been made known. But we know that when Christ appears, we shall be like him, for we shall see him as he is.

1 JOHN 3:2

*S*o many possibilities. We could be leaders. We could be followers. We could be artists or teachers. We could be musicians or scientists. So many things we could be! "What we will be has not yet been made known."

That's one of the many wonderful and amazing things about having children and watching them grow. All the possibilities. As each quirk of their personalities is revealed, you wonder again, *What will she become? Who will he be like? What will she do? Where will he go?*

And even though you may be well past your own childhood years, it's exciting to think the possibilities are still wide open. We are children of God. And who knows what we will be in our eternal life with Him?

There are some things we do know. We know we will be like Jesus in some way—having a new body, as Christ took on a new body when He was resurrected from the dead. We know we will be with Him.

But beyond that?

As you pray today, consider the possibilities, not just for the next life, but for the rest of this one. You are a child of God. Don't be limited by what you have or haven't been in the past. Be more now. Do more now. Live differently.

As His Own

Mordecai had taken her as his own daughter when her father and mother died.
ESTHER 2:7

The story of Esther is noted as a tale of bravery—a story about one woman having courage enough to stand up for her people. But it's interesting to go back and wonder—where did that courage come from?

Esther was adopted as a child by her older cousin, Mordecai. Mordecai was Jewish and proud of his faith. He was also proud of Esther. It's highly likely that he would have raised her in Jewish ways, teaching her the Jewish traditions—teaching her to follow the one true God. Perhaps she heard stories of other strong Jewish women—stories of Sarah and Rachel and the mother of Moses.

Who we are and who we become depends so much on the love and care we receive as children. Mordecai must have done a solid job of training Esther in her faith because when a crisis point came, Esther turned not to wealth or power but to prayer. She asked Mordecai and all her Jewish community to pray and fast for her. And deep in the rooms of the palace, she and all her attendants bowed before God and asked for His help, too.

Mothers come in many forms. Some are biological. Some are adopted. Some are actually fathers or cousins or aunts or grandparents. But no matter who it is, if the person cares and loves, if the person teaches and disciplines, if the person prays and gives, there is no telling what an amazing impact on the world they might have.

Lord, thank You for all those who have helped teach me about You. Amen. —ML

From Birth

Yet you brought me out of the womb; you made me trust in you, even at my mother's breast. From birth I was cast on you; from my mother's womb you have been my God.

PSALM 22:9–10

*B*abies trust us so completely from day one. Studies have shown that babies do hear and become familiar with certain voices that are constantly around them as they grow in the womb. So when they're finally ready to meet the world, they at least have some familiar sounds to greet them.

Perhaps one of those voices they know well is that of the Lord. Children often instinctively seem to know of and talk about God in a way that is so simple and true—as if they are talking about an old friend.

As a baby reaches out and receives nourishment from his mother, he learns that God provides. As he cries out and is then picked up, he learns that God hears. As he wiggles and smiles and receives smiles and kisses in return, he learns that God loves.

We learn to trust what we know. And we know what we can see and hear and feel. What better way for God to speak to us than through the loving touch and voices of our parents.

This makes it all the more important for us to make sure every child has a loving caregiver, and to offer care and help to every parent in need.

What can you do for a struggling parent today?

Lord, help me show Your love to every parent
and child who needs to trust You. Amen. —ML

Wait for the Lord

Though my father and mother forsake me, the LORD will receive me.
PSALM 27:10

If there is anything certain about the humans of this world, it's that they will at some point disappoint us. Even our own parents.

It might be something small—a special treat we had to skip or a present we didn't get. Or it might be something huge—abandonment or abuse. But at some point, something will happen that will cause us to feel a little less sure of our world.

Psalm 27 reads something like a list of ways in which humans might let us down or turn on us. They might attack us or start wars. They might reject or forsake us. They might oppress us or lie about us.

But through all of that, one of many things remains certain about our God—He will not disappoint us. He will embolden us with His light and salvation. He will give us a stronghold. He will make our enemies fall. He will fill our world with beauty. He will keep us safe in His shelter. He will not reject us but instead accept and welcome us. He will lead us to His goodness in the land of the living.

What do we have to do? Call on Him. Ask Him to help us. Sing and make music to Him. Be strong and take heart.

Just wait for Him.

Lord, heal me of wounds inflicted by humans and help me wait on You. Amen. —ML

I Am Content

But I have calmed and quieted myself, I am like a weaned
child with its mother; like a weaned child I am content.
PSALM 131:2

$\mathscr{A}$ great debate is probably still raging in some corner of motherland right now. It's a debate about when a breastfeeding mom should stop nursing her child. Some say when the child is old enough to ask for it plainly, then it's time to stop. Some say three years old. Some say keep going as long as you can.

At whatever stage it eventually happens, if the weaning process is done well, the child is likely to be content. Why? Because she will be getting nourishment elsewhere.

A child who is weaned doesn't stop eating. Nor does she stop growing. She just starts using a different food source. Or in most cases, many food sources. And usually these new sources provide more fuel than she can get any longer from a bottle or breast.

When we first learn about God and the world, we learn from what our parents or teachers tell us. And when we have grown in our faith and moved past what our parents have taught us or what we can learn from picture storybooks, we have another source from which to learn about God. We have His Word. We have prayer. And we have our own relationship with Him.

Lord, help me be content with the things I know. Help me
put my hope in You, now and forevermore. Amen. —ML

What We Share

Now if we are children, then we are heirs—heirs of God and co-heirs with Christ, if indeed we share in his sufferings in order that we may also share in his glory.
ROMANS 8:17

Many children have a difficult time learning to share. Indeed, to them it must seem that they just barely began to grasp the idea that they even had certain toys, when suddenly those toys were being taken out of their hands and put in another child's— accompanied by the dreaded word *share*.

But through patient repetition, we all generally grasp the idea that it's good to share. It's generous to let others have what you have—even if it's just for a limited amount of time.

Through sharing we learn something about each other and about ourselves. We learn what we like or don't like. We learn what is hard and easy to do. We learn what things have value to us and how much we value them.

Jesus shared in our sufferings through His death on the cross. And we share in a small way in His suffering when we care for others and when we are threatened or treated badly because of our faith in Him.

We will share fully in His glory when we are made whole and brought to eternal life in heaven with him. But here on earth we can share in glimpses of that glory when we rejoice over another person brought to know and love Jesus.

Lord, help me share You with others. Amen. —ML

When I Sit

You know when I sit and when I rise; you perceive my thoughts from afar.
PSALM 139:2

*E*ver have a day when you can't even remember when you last sat down? Just to sit—not to drive the car somewhere to pick up someone and drop them off somewhere else. Not to sew on a button. Not while attempting to feed a mouth that refuses every bite. Not squatting on a floor to change a diaper.

But just to sit.

Some of you may read this verse of Psalm 139 and laugh. You may think, *Well, I'm glad God knows my thoughts because I can't remember them past lunch.* Or perhaps the thought of God seeing your thoughts from afar is downright alarming. That line, along with the one a few verses down that says God knows our words before they even land on our tongues, might be just enough to send you into panic mode.

But don't panic.

God is not some giant brain cop aiming to sting you for every wrong thought or careless word that passes through your sleep-deprived mind. The real message of Psalm 139 is that God knows you. He knows you in ways you don't even know yourself, and yet He still wants to be with you.

Only someone who knows you that well and loves you that much can lead you to be better than what you are today. Will you let him lead you?

But maybe before that, you could just, possibly. . .sit.

Lord, thank You for wanting to be with me, despite my mess. Amen. —ML

What Can You Take?

Everyone comes naked from their mother's womb, and as everyone comes, so they depart
They take nothing from their toil that they can carry in their hands.
ECCLESIASTES 5:15

⌇

You can't take it with you."

Usually the word *it* in that statement is meant to refer to your possessions—your stuff. This statement is made to encourage you not to spend time acquiring more things but instead to spend it on what really matters—such as your children.

It's a good point. We bring new babies into the world and think they're perfect, just as they are. But it isn't long before we're stressing over clothing them in sweet outfits and giving them all the latest toys and making sure we pay for the best educational tools. All of which takes time and money.

But how much time do you spend thinking about what will go with you when you leave this world? How much time are you spending now to make sure your children are on the path to eternal life?

The Bible doesn't give us a lot of details about the next life, but we can take comfort in knowing a few things. First is that Jesus knows what it's like to be human. He knows what we care about and what we hold dear. Jesus also knows what we really need. And the Bible tells us that the person we will be in that new life will be whole and complete in a way we cannot be now.

But perhaps the most important thing to know is that though we can't take *it*, we can definitely take *Him*.

Lord, help me let go of the things that don't
matter and hold on tightly to You. Amen. —ML

Mysteries

As you do not know the path of the wind, or how the body is formed in a mother's womb, so you cannot understand the work of God, the Maker of all things.
ECCLESIASTES 11:5

The blob shifts and changes, light and shadow swirling at first together and then separating again. Two circular dark spaces appear for a moment and then are gone. Is that a head? Or something else? A leg jabs out. Then a hand reaches up into a space. Five fingers—clear as day.

For the untrained eye, staring at sonogram images can be like trying to figure out some strange sort of liquid puzzle, where the parts keep moving. It's always such a relief to find anything that looks familiar.

Today there are some devices that provide images that are so clear, you feel you could almost use them for your kid's preschool picture.

But no matter how clear the image or how detailed the exam or how many facts we have now gathered about the process of creating human life, there is still so much we don't know. It's still a mystery. A miracle. One egg and one sperm somehow join together to form a mind, an imagination, a heart, a soul. How does that happen?

If we cannot even figure out something that occurs right under our noses, so to speak, how can we ever claim to understand the work of God? And if we cannot understand the work of God, shouldn't we maybe think about spending a little more time with Him?

Lord, thank You for the mysteries in this world that make me want to know more. Help me know more of You. Amen. —ML

Endlessly Comforting

> *"As a mother comforts her child, so will I comfort you;*
> *and you will be comforted over Jerusalem."*
> **ISAIAH 66:13**

It starts with a squirming and wriggling. Then a squeal and a whine. Next, two little hands reach up into the cold night air and the fingers grasp for something—someone. The whine develops into a full cry. The eyes scrunch and the mouth opens wider. One big breath and then—"Mamaaaaaaa!"

But it doesn't end there. Once the toddler is out of the crib, the call continues to come. Because of a dead pet fish. A dropped ice cream cone. A smashed toe.

The toddler becomes an elementary school kid and the call still comes. Hurt feelings. Hard homework. Mean words.

The student gets older and the call still comes. Out of gas. Minor accident. Major crush.

The student waves good-bye and heads to college and the call still comes, late at night. Bad decisions. Consequences. Fears. Panic.

The adult graduates and begins a job, a marriage, a life. The call still comes. Arguments. Indecision. Regrets. Celebrations!

There are so many worries in the world. So much room for error. So much suffering. So the calls still come. And our calls still go up. "Please, God, help her." "Please, God, give me words." "Please, God, keep him safe."

It's a relief to know that our God knows how to comfort us, like a mother comforts her children. Always. Anytime. Forever.

Lord, thank You for comforting me, every time. Amen. —ML

Worthy

*"Anyone who loves their father or mother more than me is not worthy of me;
anyone who loves their son or daughter more than me is not worthy of me."*
MATTHEW 10:37

It sounds harsh somehow. Is Jesus telling us not to love our family? Is He telling us we have to reject our moms and dads?

And in some ways, His words are intentionally harsh. A few sentences prior, we read: "Do not suppose that I have come to bring peace to the earth. I did not come to bring peace, but a sword" (verse 34).

So, we're not supposed to give peace a chance?

It depends on the cost. Peace at any price? No. The peace that comes from taking up your cross and following Him? Yes.

Now some would have no problem turning their backs on their families. In fact, they already did that ages ago. But that isn't Jesus' point here. His point is that if there's anything getting in the way of you following Jesus, anything keeping you from knowing Him, anything holding you back from accepting Him as your Savior, then you need to take stock of your priorities. If worries about what your family or friends might think are holding you back, you need to let go of that. If caring for the sports schedule is keeping you from having time with Christ, then you need to cut back.

No one is worthy of Jesus. But to be made able to follow Him—to be made seaworthy to navigate the troubled waters of this life—we have to sometimes dump some extra cargo.

God, help me know what I need to let go of. Amen. —ML

Marvel

The child's father and mother marveled at what was said about him.
LUKE 2:33

$\mathcal{T}$he first time a new baby makes his or her appearance at any social event, the *oohs* and *aahs* just can't be stopped. Everyone wants to see and touch and smell and hold the little bundle. People comment on the cute clothing, the tiny shoes, and the big bows. They extend the little fingers and talk about how long they are. They wonder at the exquisite toes and miniscule toenails. They pass their fingers lightly over the soft scalp and gently squeeze the chunky elbows.

Then the eyes open and another round of praise and adoration erupts.

Why are we so amazed by babies? Is it their smallness? Their perfectly scaled-down bodies? Is it the mystery about what they must be thinking behind those big eyes and toothless grins?

Whatever the reason, the infant Jesus must have topped the charts in terms of baby marvels.

Simeon had been waiting for this day for a long time. When he saw that baby enter the temple courts, he moved toward Mary, took the child in his arms, and prayed. But instead of thanking God for tiny toes and perfect fingers, Simeon acknowledged God's fulfillment of a promise—the promise of salvation for all God's people. Not only that, but this devout Jewish man recognized that this salvation, this light would be not just for the Jews but for the Gentiles as well.

It's no wonder Mary and Joseph marveled at what was said. They knew Jesus was special—the angel had told them that. But sent to everyone?

Yes, to *every*one. Even you and me.

Lord, thank You for the miracle and wonder that babies inspire. Thank You for the miracle of Your love sent to us through baby Jesus. Amen. —ML

Scattered

"Whoever is not with me is against me,
and whoever does not gather with me scatters."
LUKE 11:23

You probably know the game of 52 Pickup. Or you may know it by another description: cleaning up after a toddler. For every two things you put away, the straggling wee one behind you gets out fifty more.

Of course they don't mean to make life difficult for anyone—they're just learning, observing, experimenting. What happens when I pull this? What's under all these clothes in the basket? Can I reach those? These must be the kinds of questions running through their very busy minds. They're curious creatures—desiring to know and feel and understand more about the world around them. They don't mean to make a mess. The mess just happens.

But Jesus wasn't talking about toddlers. He was talking about us—the grown-ups. And sometimes we don't mean to make a mess either, but we do make the decisions that lead us there. Instead of standing with Him, we go our own way. Instead of bringing our concerns about people and problems to Him, we try to reach and dig and pull on our own.

Instead of stopping to pray and ask and think, we just keep moving forward—picking up a few things and leaving a lot behind.

Let's try a different way today. Let's let Jesus lead us—even if it means a few more toddler experiments happen along the way.

Lord, please help me see the people You want me to gather to You today. Amen. —ML

A Knowing Nudge

His mother said to the servants, "Do whatever he tells you."
JOHN 2:5

It must have been a proud moment for her. She had raised this young man in the best way she could. She had given Him a good Jewish upbringing. And now He was starting out on His own—beginning His ministry and already gathering followers. But she couldn't have known all that would unfold in the next few years. In this moment, all she knew was that she had a remarkable son, who was capable of solving problems no one else could.

So when they were at a community event, and Mary saw that the host would be put in an awkward, even dishonoring, position, she did what any mother in her situation would do. She gave her son a nudge. "They have no more wine," she said (verse 3). Jesus seemed reluctant to solve this particular problem, yet His mother must have been sure of her son, because she told the servants, "Do whatever he tells you."

It's amazing to raise little humans who become big humans, and to see the way the Father works in them. So much of who they are and who they become is out of our hands, but it's wonderful to celebrate and thank God for these little moments of knowing. These moments when we are certain we know them—and that they will respond to our nudge.

God, thank You for little moments of understanding between me and my child. Amen. —M

Joined Together

They all joined together constantly in prayer, along with the
women and Mary the mother of Jesus, and with his brothers.
ACTS 1:14

If motherhood does nothing else for us, it surely increases our prayer life. From the moment they take their first breath until the moment we take our last, we pray for our children. Even those moms who aren't really sure God is listening still cry out for help. We worry about their growth, their health, their understanding of the world, their friends. . .about everything!

But can you imagine what Mary must have been praying about in those days after Jesus, her child, was taken up into the sky?

Of course, He had been on His own for quite some time at that point. But it seemed she had continued to be in His life. He certainly didn't reject her. Even on the cross, He was asking for her to be taken care of.

She must have grieved His suffering on the cross. And she must have rejoiced when He rose from the dead. But now—after He just disappeared?

Perhaps they had said their good-byes. Perhaps He took a moment in those days leading up to His ascension to have one last walk with His mother.

We can't know. All we know is that she was there with her family, there with all the ones closest to Him. Perhaps she just wanted to feel joined together with Jesus, and to be praying for her child, one last time.

Lord, thank You for listening to us even when we don't
know what to say or what to do next. Amen. —ML

The Others

Greet Rufus, chosen in the Lord, and his mother, who has been a mother to me, too.
ROMANS 16:13

*S*ome of us have children from a variety of families. No, not adopted. Not officially. But they belong to us in a special way.

Many mothers mother others. We take care of the kid down the street, whose parents always seem to be busy. Or the kid up the street whose mom is sick. We take care of the kids our kids bring home and invite over and go out with.

Sometimes it's not all that convenient. Sometimes it's pretty costly—all those kids are hungry! Sometimes it doesn't seem worth it.

But Jesus said, "If anyone gives even a cup of cold water to one of these little ones who is my disciple, truly I tell you, that person will certainly not lose their reward" (Matthew 10:42).

So go ahead. Reach out. Give an extra hug. Open up the snack drawer. Order another pizza. Spend a little more time. Stretch your heart a bit further and your arm a bit wider.

After all, you never know who that little kid you wave to every day may grow up to be. Maybe he'll be a doctor someday. Or maybe your boss! Maybe even the president. Or maybe he'll be someone—like Paul—who goes and tells the world about Jesus. Maybe because some nice lady once took the time to tell that story to him.

God, thank You for the opportunity to show Your love to others.
Help me take hold of it willingly and with grace. Amen. —ML

Faithful Generations

I am reminded of your sincere faith, which first lived in your grandmother
Lois and in your mother Eunice and, I am persuaded, now lives in you also.
2 TIMOTHY 1:5

The quilt is worn. There are holes torn along its edges. There are threads sticking out where they ought to be tucked in. There are a few stains here and there—hot chocolate drops, spaghetti sauce, a bit of nail polish.

It certainly doesn't look as perfect as it once did, when Grandmother put the last stitch in. But it's softer than it was then—made so by the many times little hands pulled it up around a chilly neck, or the times it was snuggled with on sick tummy days, or the times it was laid out for a picnic with various stuffed animal friends. The quilt has helped keep you warm; it has comforted your child when someone went away; and even now you sniff it to get a whiff of the blessed past and the good memories that come with it.

A lot of work went into that quilt. A lot of thought was given to the colors and patterns that would go together. A lot of time was spent putting in every stitch. And every minute was worth it to create this family heirloom that will be passed down for generations.

Our faith can be like that quilt. A lot of time is spent holding it together, but in the end we have something that is a comfort for generations. And it's worth every minute.

God, thank You for families of faith and the examples we have in our elders. Amen. —ML

Mommy Truce

A heart at peace gives life to the body, but envy rots the bones.
PROVERBS 14:30

Who knows when the mommy wars started, or why or how. But somewhere along the way, moms started picking at each other. Name a subject, and there has probably been a veritable dissertation of comments written about it from all sides and from all kinds of mothers: styles of clothing, whether or not to breastfeed, disciplining kids in public, the kinds of discipline used, sleep methods or lack thereof, homeschooling or public schooling or no schooling, even whether babies should wear socks or not. The discussions are endless. And so are the unkind remarks.

Maybe we just don't get out enough. Maybe we just are so starved for adult conversation that we'll take it in any form. Or maybe we are just a little bit envious. Jealous of the moms who look like they have it all together; or the ones who can afford all the best camps; or the ones who seem to have enough time to cook elaborate packed lunches, craft beautiful scrapbooks, and help every child memorize the Declaration of Independence—all before noon.

Just before you hit send on that e-mail or before you post that snarky comment or before you gripe to your girlfriend, stop and pray. Ask God to help you hold your tongue. Ask God to help you see people as He sees them. Call a truce in the mommy wars and be at peace with other moms and with yourself.

God, You know my heart. Help me guard it against envy or thinking mean thoughts. Amen. —ML

Leaving Them Behind

When I was a child, I talked like a child,
I thought like a child, I reasoned like a child.
1 CORINTHIANS 13:11

Time to confess. How many moms out there have actually deliberately not corrected a child's mispronunciation of a word because it just sounded so doggone cute?

When our children graduate from baby babble to speaking in sentences, we rejoice in being able to understand their wants and needs better. But at each stage, moms grieve just a little over those lost, sweet, swapped consonants or stumbled-over syllables. "Mama, can I have some wawa pease?" "Mama, me hungee! Can we have pasgetti?"

However, it certainly would be silly to want our children to continue to talk like babies for the rest of their lives. Everyone has to grow up at some point. That's exactly how it should be. But sometimes we hang on to childish ways longer than we should. Like a child, we want what we want and don't consider much about how our wants might conflict with someone else's needs. We just can't see that far.

But we know enough, even in our partial and cloudy knowledge, to know that we need God. In order to love like Him, to give like Him, and to live like Him, we have to call on Him.

Lord, help me remember that we are all still growing—none of us is complete.
Help me identify childish behavior in myself and leave it behind me. Amen. —ML

Ancient Comfort

I remember, Lord, your ancient laws, and I find comfort in them.
PSALM 119:52

Children love to run. They especially love to run away from their parents. Go to any fair, mall, wedding reception, or other crowded venue, and you are likely at some point to see a small ball of energy go flying past your knees. And two seconds later, a flapping parent follows, calling the name of the little runaway.

But set that same child down in the middle of the crowd and walk away a few steps—just out of sight—and you'll get an interesting response. Usually that child will begin to look around with a panicked expression and immediately cry for mommy.

Humans need structure. As much as we long to be free, we long for guidelines. Having a framework of some kind means someone is watching out for us. Someone cares. Someone is there.

When we read the words of the Bible, we see plainly in those pages a God who is watching out for us. A God who cares. A God who is there. We can look into His law and understand that every word is there for a purpose. In every line, He was thinking about His children—about us.

He never leaves us alone. And He has never left any of us alone. For thousands of years, He has been there for His children. He always stays within sight, so we never have to panic. He is always only a prayer away.

Lord, thank You for leaving Your ancient wisdom for us in a form we can understand. And thank You for letting us know You are there. Amen. —ML

Better Together

Two are better than one, because they have a good return for their labor:
If either of them falls down, one can help the other up.
ECCLESIASTES 4:9–10

Strong families are made of strong partnerships. At the heart of the family is the husband and wife—holding it all together, taking turns, sharing the work. Then there are partnerships between siblings—they play with each other, follow each other, and depend on each other. Finally, there are partnerships between parents and their children.

A mother and child partnership doesn't always succeed in getting much work accomplished. A mother baking a cake on her own could certainly do it a lot faster (and probably with less mess). Trips to the store would be a lot shorter. And any type of organization would doubtless be more efficient without a set of little, busy hands adding to the chaos. But there is something good that comes out of sharing a task. In fact, there are many good things that come out of it: laughter, friendship, warm memories, patience, and understanding, to name a few.

But the strongest families also cultivate partnerships with God. So that if, by some chance, everyone falls down at the same time, we can reach out to Him and receive help to get up again.

Lord, thank You for showing us that we need each other. Help me remember to be patient and know that we are better together. Amen. —ML

Renewed

Those who hope in the Lord will renew their strength.
ISAIAH 40:31

❧

*H*ow was your yesterday? Good or bad or somewhere in the middle?

What about last week? Any mistakes in it? Any words you wish you would not have said? Were there times you wish you could erase? Conversations that didn't go the way you planned?

All of us have bad days. Sometimes the work we have to do is just too much. Sometimes we just don't feel that well. Sometimes we're exhausted.

And most of the time, the children just won't see this. They will decide that is the day to be obstinate or overly active. They will pick that day to push all your buttons.

It's a terrible combination—you are at your weakest and they seem filled with energy.

But don't fret. Ask forgiveness instead. Start with your Father then ask the children, too. Then start this day renewed.

Children need to know that sometimes people get tired. They need to learn what it means to have compassion for those who are feeling weak. They need to exercise compassion for you—their mom. And they need to learn to forgive.

God promises us that He will never "grow tired or weary" of us, and "his understanding no one can fathom" (verse 28). No matter how weak we become, He is able to keep supplying us with strength—enough for this life and the life to come.

Lord, sometimes I am so tired. Thank You for renewing me. Amen. —ML

Shine

Then you will shine among them like stars in the
sky as you hold firmly to the word of life.
PHILIPPIANS 2:15–16

There's a layer of dust on the windowsill that the children have drawn faces in. The dining room table is covered with papers. The bookshelves are in disarray. Toys have crept into every corner. A single sock adorns a chair.

You look in the mirror and see lines and shadows, sagging skin and graying hairs. You can't seem to quite muster a smile.

Then a child comes in and wraps his arms around you in a big squeeze. And suddenly your face lights up and you find your shine!

God wants us to be like small children—"blameless and pure" and "without fault in a warped and crooked generation" (verse 15). It seems like a tall order, but He gives us a hint as to how to get there: "Do everything without grumbling or arguing" (verse 14).

God wants our actions to stand out in a world that doesn't know Him. It doesn't matter if we don't feel so shiny, or if our house is looking a little dim and dusty. If we "hold firmly" to His Word and hold onto our tongues, we can be the example He wants us to be. Some days it will be hard not to grumble and argue, but if all it takes is a little self-control to become a shining star, then it is definitely worth the effort! And the best part is, God will help us find our shine—we only have to ask.

Lord, please help me be a shining light out in
the world and draw people to You. Amen. —ML

Eat and Rejoice

*There, in the presence of the L*ORD *your God, you and your families shall eat and shall rejoice in everything you have put your hand to, because the L*ORD *your God has blessed you.*

DEUTERONOMY 12:7

There are days when it seems like getting everyone gathered around the table for family dinner is like herding butterflies—everyone is flitting about in different directions. But it's important to make an effort to come together as a family every day.

Family mealtime is a special time to celebrate our small victories—a hard-earned B on a dreaded test, a completed furniture painting project, a productive day in the office, or a fly ball caught with ease. It's a few minutes where we can sit together and look into each other's eyes. It's a safe place to connect and touch base.

It's also a place to connect to God. When we thank our God for our blessings, we emphasize to our kids that we are not the ones in control, that we owe everything to God. In a subtle way we are able to demonstrate that we need to be grateful for what we have, because there are so many who have so little.

It can also be a place to let others see God in your lives. Invite other friends and their families. Rejoice together over all the good things that have happened. Rejoice in simply being together.

God, we rejoice in Your many blessings today. Thank You so much! Amen. —ML

Because

"Because I live, you also will live."
JOHN 14:19

You're going to be okay.

Let's read that again. You're going to be okay.

Whatever hard thing you are going through right now, whatever trial, whatever mess you are staring at, whatever latest madness your children have brought to you, whatever migraine is weighing on you—you're going to be okay.

Why?

Because Jesus said so.

Jesus said, "Because I live, you also will live."

Now if anyone else had said that, it would have been easy to brush them off. Yeah, sure. You live, I live, we are all alive. Great.

But this is Jesus we're talking about. Jesus the Son of God. Emmanuel. Jesus the Messiah. Lord Jesus Christ. King of kings. Lord of lords. Alpha and Omega. The Way. The Truth. The Life.

The Life.

This Jesus says we will live. He says we will live—just like He lives now. This Jesus who hung on a cross and suffered severe pain; this man who faced death for us, who was laid in a tomb for three days; this Jesus who defeated death and rose again and lives even now, seated at the right hand of His Father in heaven—this is the guy who said, "Because I live, you also will live."

You're going to be more than okay.

You're going to be eternally okay. Just ask Him.

Lord Jesus, thank You for defeating death for us so we can live fully in You. Amen. —ML

Laughing through Tears

Even in laughter the heart may ache, and rejoicing may end in grief.
PROVERBS 14:13

Isn't it satisfying to have a God who knows us so completely?

In His Word we can find, time and time again, examples of the ways He intimately knows the human experience. God knows what our daily lives are like. He knows all of the emotions we go through in any given day. That's why we need to continue to talk with Him—there is no one—no counselor, no pastor—who knows us so completely as our heavenly Father.

Have you ever had to take a deep breath and face the bedtime routine after receiving devastating news? Even as you sing a lullaby and tickle those little bellies and tuck in their blankets, your heart aches with grief. You laugh at their chuckles and giggles—you can't help it. But with the laughter, a few tears escape and make a path down your cheek onto your child's pillow as you kiss the smooth forehead and rub it with your own furrowed one.

How many times have mothers started out celebrating with joy over some friend's accomplishment or a child's happy achievement, only to end up in tears? Sometimes they are happy tears. Other times they are tears that pay tribute to the days that we have lost or to the time we can't get back. Sometimes the joy reminds us of others who are suffering.

No matter what face we put on for others, God knows our hearts. And that alone is a great comfort.

God, thank You for knowing me so well. Please help me remember I can always talk to You. Amen. —ML

Inside the Fish

From inside the fish Jonah prayed to the LORD his God.
JONAH 2:1

The story of Jonah is fascinating for many reasons. Not least of which, of course, is the whole man-swallowed-alive-by-a-huge-fish thing.

But one remarkable fact that often gets overlooked in this story is that Jonah prayed while he was still in the big fish's belly. And he didn't pray, "Oh God, get me out of here!" No, he prayed, "Thank You, God, for saving me!" He thanked God for the weirdest rescue of all time—being slurped into the slimy stomach of super seafood. He thanked God for giving him a second chance.

It's a good reminder to us. We don't need to wait till the crisis is over to thank God. We don't need to clean up the post-potluck dishes or wait till the crying stops or postpone until the car is towed away. We can stop right now, in whatever sticky situation we are sitting in, and acknowledge the place God has in our lives. We can hold on tight to our children and say, "Let's thank God that He's here for us even in the middle of this storm."

Imagine what an amazing memory that will be for your kids as they grow and face their own oceans of troubles! God is here for us—even when the view isn't pretty, when the fog hasn't cleared, and when we still don't know where to go. He is here, and He will remember us.

God, thank You for listening to my cry, even in the depths of distress. Amen. —ML

Parenting Lessons

Then Manoah prayed to the Lord: *"Pardon your servant, Lord. I beg you to let the man of God you sent to us come again to teach us how to bring up the boy who is to be born."*
JUDGES 13:8

*Y*ou've got to give Manoah some credit—he's got guts. An angel actually appears to his wife and tells her she is going to give birth (after being barren for some time). That would be amazing enough for most people. But perhaps Manoah's reaction was not one of joy or happy surprise. The Bible doesn't tell us how long the couple had lived without children. It's possible Manoah had become quite content with their living situation. Perhaps the father-to-be was just a bit afraid of this new little person coming to his house!

So Manoah asked God to send the angel back. And when you think about it, it's not such a bad idea. Shouldn't we all be asking God to teach us how to bring up our kids? And what better time to make that request than before the child is even born?

Perhaps it would be a bit disconcerting to have an angel show up on the doorstep to begin teaching Parenting 101, but who among us wouldn't like to have some concrete guidance in this area of our lives? Thankfully, God has provided us much wisdom in His Word about how to live with and love human beings—which is mainly what the business of parenting is all about. And His parenting hotline is open 24/7 for our questions, concerns, and 3:00 a.m. panic attacks.

Lord, You are the perfect parent. Guide me through my imperfection. Amen. —ML

Brokenhearted

*The righteous cry out, and the L*ORD *hears them; he delivers them from all their troubl*
*The L*ORD *is close to the brokenhearted and saves those who are crushed in spirit.*
PSALM 34:17–18

*W*hen you're young and in love for the first time, or even just in like, that moment
when you discover that your major crush is crushing on someone else is, well,
crushing. There you were, with visions of bridal gowns and happy children in your
head (never mind being just thirteen), and suddenly the scene goes black. Mr. Perfect
has walked right out of the picture.

It's heartbreaking.

But a whole other level of heartbreak is having to watch your child go through th
same thing.

Maybe for your kid it's not a crush. Maybe it's just being left out of the games.
Maybe it's being called a mean name. Maybe it's being treated badly simply because o
the way he or she looks.

Whatever that first injury is, it can be gut-wrenching to watch it from afar as a
parent and not really be able to do anything to make it go away. The hurts will come.
We cannot shield our children from them all.

It's such a relief to know that our Lord feels this pain with us. We can tell Him ou
troubles, and He will come close to our children. He will heal their spirits and mend
their hearts. He will lift them up out of these troubles—and no doubt they will be
even stronger than before.

God our Father, please mend my children's heart wounds and lift their spirits. Amen. —ML

Like Rain

Let my teaching fall like rain and my words descend like dew,
like showers on new grass, like abundant rain on tender plants.
DEUTERONOMY 32:2

Moses spoke these words as part of a song of praise to God that he delivered to the people just before his death. He wanted what he had to say to remain with the listeners. He wanted them to be refreshed and enlivened.

It's a prayer we would do well to repeat whenever we're facing difficult conversations with our children. New grass soaks up water eagerly. It needs the water to help it extend roots quickly and grab hold of the soil. But the young plants also need the water to keep them standing upright and to complete the process of making fuel for themselves.

The young plants accept the water readily because that is just the time when they need it. God knows when our children's hearts are ready to accept certain messages as well. He knows what words of advice or rebuke or encouragement they need to hear. He knows the best time for us to deliver those words.

Ask God to guide you. Ask Him to shed light on opportunities to speak with your children about upcoming decisions or to talk with them about the consequences of their actions. Let Him lead you naturally into talks with your kids that will help you and them understand the state of their souls.

Lord show me the best time to talk with my kids. Amen. —ML

Puzzled

Oh, the depth of the riches of the wisdom and knowledge of God!
How unsearchable his judgments, and his paths beyond tracing out!
ROMANS 11:33

Puzzles can be mind-twisting. Just when you think you have a section solved, you realize one of the parts doesn't quite fit and the assumptions you were making based on that one piece all now have to be reconsidered.

Figuring out our children's wants and needs can sometimes be equally puzzling. Just when we think we've figured them out, they change their minds or reveal the error in our conclusions.

God is used to solving hard puzzles though. In fact, He created all of them. The depth of His ability to understand and piece together and solve is beyond our comprehension. Even the trickiest logic puzzle or the most complex math equation could not stump our Lord.

We can trust Him to give us the knowledge we need at the appropriate times. We can rely on His wisdom.

Now that doesn't mean He will always provide us with all the answers exactly when we want them. Anyone who's been raising children for very long can tell you that. We're often stumped. We're frequently confused. We're regularly surprised. But there's a lot of encouragement in knowing that Jesus is not only the answer to many of our problems, He also knows the answer to any puzzle we could ever encounter. Even if it's math.

Oh God, I am in awe of Your limitless knowledge.
Please share Your wisdom with me when I need it. Amen. —ML

End of the World

Nation will rise against nation, and kingdom against kingdom. There will be famines and earthquakes in various places. All these are the beginning of birth pains.
MATTHEW 24:7–8

In case you ever wondered if our Lord and Savior understands the pain of childbirth, just read this passage. Nations and kingdoms clash! There's famine and earthquakes! And that, friends, is just the beginning of birth pains!

Seriously, though, Jesus made an apt analogy here when He was talking about the end of the world as we know it. Having a baby in many ways does mark an incomparable shift.

One day you're an adult, able to make decisions about where you want to go and when you want to go there. The next day your schedule is suddenly and wholly taken over by a tiny ruler in a diaper. Everything changes.

And those changes most definitely begin when your body announces that the baby you've been carrying for nine months is ready to move. A significant shift happens somewhere deep inside—a fault line cracks. Body organs and systems clash. Waves of pain and nausea and love and fear and anxiety and joy and. . .*everything* flow through your core. And all of that is just the beginning of a wild ride we call parenthood.

But as for the end of the world, as Jesus said, "You do not know on what day your Lord will come" (verse 42). All we can do is have our hearts ready. Lay all your worries on Jesus—He will take care of you.

Lord, I'm glad You understand the whole range of human experience. Help me remember there's nothing I can't talk to You about. Amen. —ML

Your Will

He went away a second time and prayed, "My Father, if it is not possible for this cup to be taken away unless I drink it, may your will be done."

MATTHEW 26:42

It's hard to imagine a harder prayer was ever prayed than this one: "Your will be done."

When you don't get the job you want. "Your will be done."

When someone betrays you but doesn't seem to pay any consequences. "Your will be done."

When you have to swallow your pride and say I'm sorry. "Your will be done."

When you make a costly mistake and your family hurts because of it. "Your will be done."

When the doctor's news isn't good. "Your will be done."

When the pain is too hard to bear. "Your will be done."

When your child is lying on a hospital bed. "Your will be done."

When the learning isn't easy. "Your will be done."

When the teachers don't seem to understand. "Your will be done."

When you're being mistreated because of your faith in Christ. "Your will be done."

When your enemies seem to get all the breaks. "Your will be done."

There may be a thousand times as a mother when you would rather pray anything other than this prayer. But in every one of those times, Jesus will be kneeling right there with you, gritting His teeth, sweat streaming down His brow, and holding on tight to your hand and praying with you. "Father, may your will be done."

Lord, help me be able to pray this prayer and really mean it. Your will be done. Amen. —M

Meditate

Blessed is the one. . .whose delight is in the law of the LORD,
and who meditates on his law day and night.
PSALM 1:1—2

A beautiful way to pray is to pray through God's Word. You can do this with any book—Psalms especially lends itself to this kind of use. But for a real challenge, open your Bible to any of the books that give the law of God. Or turn to one of Paul's letters where he's laying out how we ought to live and what we should do as Christians.

Praying through words like these will give you new perspective on God's laws. Words that you've heard again and again may speak to you in a different way.

Ask God to help you obey His laws. With each verse, make your request be for understanding of the law you are about to read. Then ask God to help you see where this law makes a difference in your life as a mother.

Not all of God's laws in the Old Testament were meant for us as modern-day Christians (and not ancient Jews) to follow word by word, of course. However, reading over books such as Leviticus helps to paint the story of God's love for His people. Among all the many laws laid out there, we see the pattern unfolding again and again of human inadequacy and rebellion, and of God's pursuit of the human heart. We see His grace displayed in all the gritty details. And we will definitely be blessed by that.

Lord, help me be someone who delights in Your law. Amen. —ML

Firm Footing

The LORD makes firm the steps of the one who delights in him; though he may stumble, he will not fall, for the LORD upholds him with his hand.

PSALM 37:23–24

The little body scrambled up the steep, rocky path like a baby mountain goat—all arms and legs and fearlessness. The mother came quickly behind, or as quick as she could go. Her steps were uncertain, faltering. Her weight shifted and her foot slid on a gravelly bit along the path, but somehow she was able to keep from stumbling and made it to the top of the path, where her four-year-old jumped up and down to greet her. "You made it, Mommy!" She sat heavily in the grass at her little one's side—no longer having the heart to deliver the stern message of rebuke she had in mind just minutes ago. The moment was past. Everyone was safe. Thank You, God!

It is supremely reassuring to know that, if we place our hearts in God's hands, He will make our steps firm. Even if our path is rocky or slippery or dangerous—He will keep us from falling down all together. He is able to give us balance—to steady our nerves and strengthen our muscles.

However, the promise is not that He will remove all the obstacles or make the path completely easy. Many times in the Bible we are told that our way is going to be hard. But if we ask Him, God is able to keep us walking steadily forward—making progress, no matter how slow.

Lord, I pray You will always go with me wherever
I go and keep making my steps firm. Amen. —ML

Family Prayers

These commandments that I give you today are to be on your hearts.
Impress them on your children. Talk about them when you sit at home and
when you walk along the road, when you lie down and when you get up.
DEUTERONOMY 6:6–7

*W*ake up. Get some coffee. Wake the children. Make some pancakes. Drink more coffee. Ask the children to eat their pancakes nicely. Stop brother from hitting sister with his fork. Drink more coffee. Stop sister from stealing brother's last bite. Demand the children eat their pancakes nicely. Drink more coffee. Nag children to clean up their plates. Make another pot of coffee.

What daily routines do you have in your family? Do you have certain waking up or going to bed traditions? Do you read the Bible together or say prayers together?

In one of the verses of the Bible that gives specific instructions to parents, Moses tells the Israelites to be sure to talk about God's commandments at every opportunity. In the morning. In the evening. Whether just sitting around in the living room or taking a walk. These commandments were to be part of them; and so, speaking about them would have been a natural thing to do.

Speaking about God's will for us should be a natural part of family life. One of the easiest ways to do this is to pray together. In the morning before you head out for your individual schedules, at dinnertime around the table, or at night as you tuck them into bed—make family prayer an everyday routine.

Lord, help me make room for prayer as a
daily part of my family's life together. Amen. —ML

No Greater Joy

I have no greater joy than to hear that my children are walking in the truth.
3 JOHN 1:4

One of the most frustrating parts of being a parent is that there are no guarantees. Some mothers pour their whole lives into their children and provide them with all kinds of healthy nourishment. Then some of those children completely rebel and make terrible life choices. Some mothers are busy and perhaps ignore their children a little too much—then those children grow up to be perfectly successful doctors and lawyers, with well-adjusted family lives of their own.

All we can do is give it our best and pray. Pray a lot. But that makes it all the more gratifying to hear others praise our children and to see our children grow into responsible, mature human beings. And there is certainly no better news as a parent—no greater joy—than to find out our children are following Christ with their whole hearts and walking in the path Jesus has set out for them.

In John's letter to his friend Gaius, he writes much as we might to one of our grown children: "I pray that you may enjoy good health and that all may go well with you, even as your soul is getting along well." If we want to have the joy of children following in the truth, it would be a good idea to make the state of their spiritual health as natural in our conversations as saying, "How are you feeling today?" We need to remember to ask our children how their souls are getting along—and to pray continually that God helps them to get along well.

Lord, bless me with the joy of children who follow You!
Help me encourage them to continue walking in Your truth. Amen. —ML

Mercy

When the kindness and love of God our Savior appeared, he saved us, not because of righteous things we had done, but because of his mercy.
TITUS 3:4–5

It happens. Our kids mess up. We come in, do our jobs: we deliver the discipline and tell them how they have disappointed us. Then we leave again, shaking our heads.

It's easy at times to forget that we were kids once, too. We made stupid decisions. We acted on our feelings. We moved too fast. We didn't listen. And we didn't always learn from our mistakes.

Before we let our anger get out of control, before we speak with a little too much of an edge or have bad thoughts about the state of our children's brains, it might be a good exercise to remember one of the stupidest things we ever did as kids. Consider that even though we made those awful choices, God let us keep on living in His world. He even let us out to associate with other humans once in a while (after our parents were done grounding us, that is).

Before you go to lay down the law, take a deep breath. Then pray. Ask God to remind you of your own shortcomings. Ask Him to give you a crystal clear picture of His mercy. Then go and talk to your child with that picture fresh in your head.

None of us is righteous. We all do stupid things. Even us grown-ups. Thank God for His great and endless mercy!

Lord, thank You for being merciful to me. Help me be merciful to others, especially my own family. Amen. —ML

One

All the believers were one in heart and mind. No one claimed that any of their possessions was their own, but they shared everything they had.

ACTS 4:32

---

*R*ead that verse above again, but this time put your family name in the part where it says "all the believers." "The Caldwells were one in heart and mind." "The Lewises were one in heart and mind. . . . They shared everything they had."

If your family is like most, this isn't always the case. Children learn that favorite expression "Mine!" very quickly, and it can take a long while for them to get good at the exercise of sharing. Some kids even write their names on their favorite foods in the refrigerator so they can be sure to eat them later.

And what about being one in heart and mind? Does this mean we all have to agree on what TV show to watch?

The likelihood of achieving this level of family unity seems small, but with God, all things are possible. We can start with little goals—like going through our belongings and giving away gently used items that we don't really need. We can have children share certain toys instead of buying one for each person. We can invest more in family experiences than we do in stuff we own and keep for ourselves. And we can make family giving goals, do service projects together, or even go on mission trips as a family.

So if your children are currently still in the "Mine!" phase, don't despair! Ask God to show how you can be an example of generosity to your family. He won't let you down!

Lord, help me cultivate a spirit of sharing in my family. Amen. —ML

Leading to Peace

Let us therefore make every effort to do what
leads to peace and to mutual edification.
ROMANS 14:19

In this part of his letter to the Romans, Paul takes some time to address the issue of people with different beliefs and religious practices. The kinds of things he speaks of in Romans 14:1–18 are the stuff of serious religious disputes among some people, even to this day. And the main point Paul makes is—don't worry about these issues, just think of others first. He says the kingdom of God is "not a matter of eating and drinking, but of righteousness, peace and joy in the Holy Spirit" (verse 17).

There is a lot of division in our world today. People want to hold on tightly to their various cultures, traditions, and values. That can be a good thing—but not if it causes followers of Christ to fight with and hurt one another.

Check your heart. Are you holding on a bit too tightly to certain traditions or beliefs that are not really essential to believing in Jesus? Are you displaying a spirit of judgment toward those who practice Christianity in a way that looks different from what you do?

It can be hard to accept change. But Paul urges us to live in a way that leads away from division and toward peace. Away from hurting one another and toward building each other up. Let's make Paul's plea in verse 19 part of our daily prayer lives, and we'll see where it leads us!

Lord, help me lead my family to peace and mutual edification. Amen. —ML

Baggage

Carry each other's burdens, and in this way you will fulfill the law of Christ.
GALATIANS 6:2

When we think of carrying each other's burdens, we may think of helping people with some hard chore, bringing meals to a sick friend, or helping someone move into a new house. A lot of people find these acts of service to be rewarding and even fun.

But the context of this verse is something that most people would not sign up for so readily. Paul is talking to the Galatians about being there for people when a brother or sister in Christ is caught in a sin.

Haven't seen a sign-up sheet for that at church lately, have you?

It can be touchy and complicated to deal with human hearts caught up in sin. And yet, this is probably the greatest responsibility we have as Christians, and especially as Christian moms.

Confronting someone about their bad choices is not fun. Sticking around to make people feel loved and wanted, even when they've hurt you or someone else you love, can seem like too much. But that's why we aren't supposed to do it alone. We're supposed to call on God and each other.

We were designed to carry each other's baggage—no matter how messy it is. Nowhere in the Bible does it say, "Keep your family sins a secret. Be sure to hold all that in." No. Instead we are to talk to one another, to get wise counsel, to have accountability partners. That's the way to restoration and wholeness in Christ.

Lord, give me courage to speak to those who are stuck in sin,
and give me patience to help lead them to restoration in You. Amen. —ML

Not Everyone

Pray that we may be delivered from wicked
and evil people, for not everyone has faith.
2 THESSALONIANS 3:2

Not everyone has faith. That seems like something of an understatement these days. Even the people who claim to have faith are not always trustworthy. It's hard to let your kids out to play in a world with so much uncertainty. If you let the "what ifs" start, you probably won't ever let them leave their bedroom closets—much less bike down the street on their own.

It's good to be wise and alert about the dangers that exist in our communities, but it's important that we don't let these fears keep us from showing God's love to the people around us. And we need to let our kids see us doing that, too.

So what do we do? Pray. Pray often. Enlist others for prayer support. Pray for protection against those who are bent on wicked deeds. Pray for the ability to see those who pretend to follow Jesus but really only follow their own desires.

But while you're at it, pray for those nonbelievers, too. The God we serve is not only big enough to protect us, He is merciful enough to reach out to the hardest hearts and break them at last.

Lord, help me resist worrying about things I cannot control.
Help me instead act on the things that You show me to do. Amen. —ML

Son Though He Was

During the days of Jesus' life on earth, he offered up prayers and petitions with fervent cries and tears to the one who could save him from death, and he was heard because of his reverent submission.
HEBREWS 5:7

*W*hat do you see when you picture Jesus? Do you see the chiseled face with flowing locks who looks out at us from many classic European works of art? Do you see a Middle Eastern man with dark skin and a dark beard? Do you see smiling, gentle eyes or a frowning, angry brow?

Do you see a lonely man, bent over onto the ground, grasping His head and rubbing away the tears that are coming too quickly to stop? Do you see a boy crying out to His Father?

Chances are, you've found yourself in that pose of desperation at least once. You've been the one begging for God to stop whatever suffering was about to occur. Your tears have streamed down your face as you called out again and again: "Please, God. Please, God. Please, God."

Even Jesus, Son of God though He was, King of kings though He was, Lord Almighty though He was, came to that place of reverent and sorrowful submission before the God of the universe. It's hard for us to wrap our minds around this moment. But God wanted us to see it. He wanted us to see that Jesus practiced obedience in what He suffered. He wanted us to see a real picture of Jesus—our brother Jesus, our friend Jesus, our fellow sufferer Jesus. This is the Jesus we need to show to our children, too.

Lord, I don't even know how to thank You for coming to earth to suffer with us. But thank You anyway. Amen. —ML

Carried Away

Do not be carried away by all kinds of strange teachings.
HEBREWS 13:9

Is there any other category of self-help books that is as vast and varied as that of the parenting section? It seems like there is a method, technique, or philosophy for every aspect of raising children, from what they eat for breakfast to what they wear to bed. For first-time parents in particular, the amount of information—or in some cases, misinformation—is absolutely overwhelming!

If you don't know exactly what you're doing, it's easy to be swayed by the loudest voice or the latest trend. The writer of Hebrews knew this. His advice about not being carried away is sandwiched between two very significant points:

1. Jesus Christ is always the same.

2. Grace is good.

First, remember that Jesus is the same today as He was when He came to earth as a baby boy. He does not change with the times. He is beyond all trends. His words are as true today as they were two thousand years ago.

Second, it's good to let your heart be strengthened by grace. The certainty of God's forgiveness gives us the confidence to love others with our whole hearts. We can step out in faith, knowing He will guide us when we ask Him to, and He will love us no matter what.

Lord, I want You to be my teacher. Guard my heart
and mind from being swayed by others. Amen. —ML

Slow

With the Lord a day is like a thousand years,
and a thousand years are like a day.
2 PETER 3:8

Some days, we want the clock to speed up. Get past this hard patch. Fast-forward till our child has grown a little and is finally out of diapers or past the separation anxiety phase or moved beyond this moody moment.

Our desire is not entirely a selfish one. Awkward stages are hard for our children, too. We'd like to shield them from growing pains, unpleasant feelings, and injured self images. On some level we can see these things are good for them—but wouldn't they be just as good if they went a little faster, we wonder?

Other days, we wish that second hand would slow to a snail-like crawl. Not only that, we wish we could add some seconds on. We take ridiculous amounts of photographs—first tooth, first haircut, first lost tooth, first bike, first everything. We stare at these images on screens and will them to come to life—to bring back our babies when they really were babies, just for another few dreamy moments.

And yet at other times, we feel the slowness is stifling. The silence is too long. The confusion and wondering and praying and figuring go on and on, and still we have no answers.

But God is not slow, and He will answer us. He's just in a completely different time zone.

And sometimes, the answer lies in the waiting.

Lord, help me be patient and live in the present. Amen. —ML

Even If

"If we are thrown into the blazing furnace, the God we serve is able to deliver us from it, and he will deliver us from Your Majesty's hand."
DANIEL 3:17

Shadrach, Meshach, and Abednego were in a pickle. Some people had noticed that these three were not falling in line. They reported this to the king: "They neither serve your gods nor worship the image of gold you have set up" (verse 12).

Now the angry king was ready to throw them into the hungry flames of the furnace. But he gave them one more chance to obey his order. And they not only still refused—they declared their undying allegiance to the God they served. They had the nerve to stand there before the king and state that their God was able to save them from the furnace. "But even if he does not, we want you to know, Your Majesty, that we will not serve your gods or worship the image of gold you have set up" (verse 18).

Even if He does not. Are you an "even if" kind of believer? Or are you an "only if" type? "God, if You'll only show me some sign, I'll believe in You." "God, if You heal my mom, then I'll know You are really real." "Lord, please help me reach my child. If You'll just do that, I'll do whatever You ask."

If you are facing a challenge, ask God to help you. Then try saying, "Even if You don't, I'll still follow You." You may be surprised at how your faith can grow, even if.

God, forgive me for trying to put conditions on You.
Help me trust in You more. Amen. —ML

Wherever You Go

"I am with you and will watch over you wherever you go."
GENESIS 28:15

Moving. Packing up your life into cardboard boxes can be an utterly exhausting task. It's not just the heaviness of the boxes that wears you out—it's the heaviness of the emotions. Uncertainty about the future. Regret about the past. Sorrow, fear, love—it's hard to pack all of that into a box!

Moving with children in the mix doubles the difficulty level. Now you don't have just your own emotions to deal with, you have theirs. They might be excited or nervous, angry or glad. And it changes day to day.

What a relief it is to know that in the middle of all the sorting and folding and taping and organizing, God is right there with us. He's right there with our children, too. He knows their hearts better than we do. And He loves them with a bigger love than we could ever muster. He promises to stay with us, even after all the dust settles and the boxes are smashed flat again.

Perhaps as we move our belongings, it would be good to try to move our hearts, too. Move into a new stage of trusting our Father. Move with Him to see where He's working in our new home. Move past our worries and into His guiding hand.

Lord, watch over us as we move and grow and change.
Help us remember You are always with us. Amen. —ML

Be Stilled

Be still before the Lord and wait patiently for him.
PSALM 37:7

*P*ut away the dishcloth. Turn off the iPod. Stop sweeping. Stop typing. Close the screen. Stop running. Stop chasing. Stop fretting. Stop fidgeting.

Don't write the to-do list in your head. Don't mentally calculate how many minutes remain before supper must be started.

Sit down.

Take your shoes off and stretch out your toes. Relax your legs and let yourself droop. Lean.

Put your hands in your lap. Turn your palms up. Feel the air touching your busy fingers. Close your eyes. Shut your mouth. Open your ears. Listen.

Don't listen for a child's cry or someone's request (note: a babysitter may be required for this devotion). Don't listen for something to happen. Just listen. What do you hear?

Let your head fall back. Take a deep breath, and as you let it out, let your shoulders fall down. Or push them down if you have to. Rest.

Think of one good thing God has done for you recently. Think about how amazing it is that our great God would care about even the smallest corners of your life. Thank God for that one good thing.

Then smile.

Remember your doubts. Think about how silly it was to worry, when God has always been there for you.

Then ask God to help you with one thing that's been troubling you.

Take another deep breath. Let it out.

Be still. And know that God is in control.

Lord, help me carve out space for stillness in my life so I can hear You better. Amen. —ML

Not as the World

"Peace I leave with you; my peace I give you.
I do not give to you as the world gives."
JOHN 14:27

The world offers us so much at times. Commercials entice us with better health, whiter smiles, and prettier hair. Consultants of all kinds invite us to sample their plan for more safety, more property, and bigger bank accounts. Life coaches want to guide us into a more organized, more purposeful, and more present existence.

But all of these come with a price. Time, money, compromised priorities. Something has got to give. We really cannot have it all.

The world gives with a tag attached—it's not a gift, it's an exchange.

But when Jesus gives us peace—it's totally, 100 percent free. We don't even have to pay for shipping.

He also gives from His own supply. He says "My peace" is what He's giving us. The peace of the Son of God. The peace of the Word that was in the very beginning. The peace that can silence kings, persuade pharaohs, and calm armies. The peace that stilled His own spirit as He waited and prayed in the Garden of Gethsemane.

It's a totally, 100 percent original product. No substitutes.

So when your children are singing the latest radio hit at the top of their lungs, and the TV is blasting, and the washer is running, and the dog is barking, and the baby is crying, and the headache is pounding—stop. Just stop for one second and remember His words: "Peace I leave with you; my peace I give you."

It's totally, 100 percent available to you right now. No purchase necessary.

Lord, help me know just a little bit of Your peace today. Amen. —ML

Get Rid of the Grumble

Offer hospitality to one another without grumbling.
1 PETER 4:9

"Mom, can I have my friend over?" "Mom, can you bring snacks for the whole soccer team?" "Mom, the robotics club doesn't have a place to meet tomorrow—can't they just come here?"

You sigh as you look around your house. The dishes are still hanging out in the sink in the hopes someone might pay attention to them. The mail pile is growing into a mail mountain. The dog has overturned his food again and left a trail leading into the dining room. Juice-stained fingerprints adorn the hall walls, and someone's face has left an image smeared across the front door.

Why me? Can't someone else do it? Or if I have to do it, why is it so hard to get someone to help clean up the pre- and post-mess?

These are just some of the thoughts that flow through your brain as the long sigh escapes your lips.

But look at it this way—at least your kids still want to be around you. And they trust you to be there for them. In a weird sense, it's their way of saying they are proud of you as a mom. Because you've made them feel so comfortable, they want to extend that comfort to others.

So get rid of the grumble. Banish the anxiety for a couple hours and just do your best. Your kids will be blessed by it, and so will all their friends.

Lord, help me be a good hostess, even when I don't feel like it. Amen. —ML

Clap with the Trees

You will go out in joy and be led forth in peace; the mountains and hills will burst into song before you, and all the trees of the field will clap their hands.
ISAIAH 55:12

Is there any day more joyful than a beautiful, sunny, spring Saturday? You pack up a picnic and the kids and head to a park for family fun. The kids' feet no sooner hit the grass than they are running, running, running—like young, wild ponies in a meadow.

The very earth seems to be bursting with sound. Flowers unfurling, bees buzzing, buds pushing up, wind humming, water bubbling, and so many bird voices singing—it's impossible to count them all.

The tree branches are alive with animals. Squirrels hop and skitter and hide. Birds get busy building nests. The branches themselves sway and stretch in the delicious breeze.

And yes, they even seem to clap.

It's so lovely and triumphant, you almost expect an orchestra to appear over the hill, playing Beethoven's "Ode to Joy."

But the instruments aren't needed today. The earth itself makes music in praise of its Creator.

Why not join it?

Sing a song of praise with your children. Laugh and run. Climb a tree. Say a prayer of thanks. Paint a picture of the lovely scene. Then share your pictures with the world so they can rejoice with you.

Lord, I rejoice in You! My heart is bursting with praise for all your glorious, beautiful creation! Amen. —ML

If We Confess

If we confess our sins, he is faithful and just and will forgive
us our sins and purify us from all unrighteousness.
1 JOHN 1:9

What if you had to stop right now and list your faults? If you had to create a list of all the mistakes you've made in the past week, how long would that list be?

Yelling at the children, losing temper with the husband, lying about being too "sick" to go to the church meeting, gossiping about a neighbor's troubles. . .this list could take a while.

Many of us are pretty good at kicking ourselves for doing stupid things. Sometimes we probably even spend a little too long fretting about and rehashing all the errors we've committed.

But how often do we sit down and just honestly confess all the sins we've done? How often do you examine your life to see where sin has taken hold?

God doesn't want us to take an extended guilt trip and dwell in despair about our sinful lives. He wants us to bring those sins to Him. When we speak to Him about the things we've done that are wrong—the times we have chosen to disobey Him—He is faithful to us. He will not beat us over the head with the weight of our wrongs. He will forgive us and release us from that heaviness.

So why not come to Him every day? Be forgiven and renewed and made pure each day, and try again to do better tomorrow. That sounds like a much better plan than packing bags for a long-stay guilt trip.

God, I know You are faithful. Please clean my heart from sin today. Amen. —ML

Don't Give Up

Let us not become weary in doing good, for at the
proper time we will reap a harvest if we do not give up.
GALATIANS 6:9

*B*ack aching, bones creaking, toes cramping, neck kinking, head aching, stomach twisting. Is this some kind of torture? No. It's just a mom driving back from a long vacation.

Hold on a second, you say. Vacation? Vacation is supposed to be fun! And it is. It was. But now the return trip has begun. Everyone is tired. Everyone is cranky. Everyone is hungry and yet somehow not willing to eat any food that's available. Everyone is picking at each other.

Don't give up, sweet mama. Hold it together for a little longer. Ask God for a little more patience. Make one more attempt at family fun. Try turning up an old song really loudly and singing at the top of your lungs. Make an unexpected stop at a random fruit stand. Try a different path. Play a license plate game. Let the kids ask you anything about your younger days. Go find ice cream.

Sometimes even the fun times we have with our families seem like a lot of work. But the blessings we get from these times together are priceless. Even on the trips when everything goes wrong, memories are made and bonds grow stronger.

So don't give up. You're almost home. Just a few more miles and then you can relax in your own bed. The laundry can wait until tomorrow.

God, give me strength! Help me not only make it through this day but to do some good to others along the way. Amen. —ML

What Is Your Mountain?

Jesus looked at them and said, "With man this is impossible,
but not with God; all things are possible with God."
MARK 10:27

Many times in our lives we face events that seem impossible to overcome—a life-summit we could never hope to reach on our own. Maybe it's at work. Maybe it's a health issue, marriage, or friendship problem. Or perhaps it's connected to our children.

Do you have a healthy child who's been diagnosed with a life-threatening illness? Or a daughter who's failing in school or is suffering from depression? Or maybe your teenage son has become rebellious and has ended up spending some time in jail. There are a thousand of these "impossible" scenarios that could overwhelm us and make us want to give up the climb. The enemy of our souls—Satan—would like nothing better than for us to do that very thing. But there is hope.

Jesus encourages us by saying that with God all things are possible. With His help, what was once unimaginable can now be achieved. What a promise! What hope to cling to when the climb looks rocky, exhausting, and fraught with danger. God will guide our steps. Every footfall, every turn, every harrowing passage. He is there, helping, strengthening, loving.

What is your mountain? What is your prayer to reach the summit?

God, give me faith in Your power to save and restore. With You by my side, I can make it to the summit. You are mighty and infinitely worthy of my trust. Amen. —AH

When They Fly Away

"And surely I am with you always, to the very end of the age."
MATTHEW 28:20

*L*ittle Julie steps up into the big yellow bus for the first time. You tell yourself you'll finally have time now to read a good book and sip some tea, but all the while there are tears running down your cheeks. Your son, Marty, is packed up. He offers you a quick hug before he heads off to college. Marty has left you with an empty room in your house and a sigh that can be heard all the way to heaven.

Kids are born. They attach themselves to your heart. Then they move away. Watching them fly on their own is one of the most woeful and wonderful parts of motherhood.

And they leave behind so many questions. Will they remember to come home? Will they make good choices? Will they follow Christ and live happy, productive lives? They are all valid questions, which makes it even more important that we pray for our children no matter their ages. Ask the Lord to stay near your kids in times when they desperately call out to Him and in times when they forget Him. Pray that they will read their Bibles, attend worship services, and seek out His good counsel in all they do.

God does love us, and He will hear our prayers. So, let us place our kids in the hands of the Lord. It's the best place for them to be when they're growing up and when they fly far from home.

Father, You love my children deeply, more than I could ever imagine.
Reveal Yourself to them and guide their steps. Amen. —AH

The Only Way to Live

Being confident of this, that he who began a good work in you will carry it on to completion until the day of Christ Jesus.
PHILIPPIANS 1:6

After we become a follower of Christ, we naturally hope for growth. But sometimes our Christian walk can feel a bit like a game of Monopoly. We take three steps forward, and then just as we think we're making some sincere headway, we find ourselves taking five steps backward. These life setbacks might come from various circumstances that arise from living in a fallen world or simply because of our own sinful actions.

We want to be good role models for our kids, so how can we show them the way it's done?

We can pray every day that the Lord will carry to completion the good work He started in us the day we accepted Christ as Lord. This takes diligence to make prayer a priority. But as Christians, it is the only way to live.

In addition, we should be willing to grow. How sad to see Christians taking the same steps backward—committing the same sins over and over and over. But with a sensitivity to the stirring of the Holy Spirit and an open heart for change, then we will witness growth in our spiritual journey. And our kids will notice, too!

Lord, give me the desire and strength to pursue holiness and a closer walk with You. Help me rely on the Holy Spirit's power when I encounter temptations. Amen. —AH

Every Good Gift

*Every good and perfect gift is from above, coming down from the Father
of the heavenly lights, who does not change like shifting shadows.*
JAMES 1:17

When the house is a train wreck of toys strewn everywhere and your body aches
from chores and errands and you wonder if you'll ever have any "me" time again,
it's easy to forget that the child storming through the house is one of those good
gifts from God. When we plop down in exhaustion on the couch, we might consider
breathing a prayer to help us remember the wonder.

You mean like, "I wonder what happened to my life?" No, not quite.

Like recalling the wonder of that precious soul who has been entrusted to your
care by the almighty hand of God. You might enjoy pondering the first kiss on that
tiny hand of hers and how it wrapped itself around your finger and your heart. Or the
first time he said, "Luv yu," and darted off to play. The times she snuggled onto your
lap with total confidence that she would find love there in your arms. The times he hit
the ball out of the park and he looked into the stands to make sure you were watching.
There are a thousand wonders to remember. A thousand reasons to thank God for this
good gift.

When harried, let us pray for the wonder to return. It's right there, even amid the
clutter and the chaos.

Father, how can I begin to thank You for my children? When my life feels like it's
unraveling, help me pause and remember the wonder of it all. Amen. —AH

This Worthy Aspiration

She speaks with wisdom, and faithful instruction is on her tongue. She watches over the affairs of her household and does not eat the bread of idleness. Her children arise and call her blessed; her husband also, and he praises her: "Many women do noble things, but you surpass them all."

PROVERBS 31:26–29

There has been a lot of talk about the "Proverbs 31 Woman" in recent years. A portion of this chapter in Proverbs has been provided, and it gives us a look at what this kind of woman would be like. Wow, pretty intimidating, right? One might even be tempted to say that this is a portrait of womanhood and motherhood that would be impossible to live out. At least on this side of heaven.

But as we take a closer look at these verses, wouldn't we secretly want to be this kind of a woman and mom? Wouldn't she be the kind of friend we would like to have?

So how could we hope to ever achieve this worthy aspiration?

Through prayer and the power of the Holy Spirit. Sound too simplistic? The world would say yes, but not God. Perhaps the changes won't come all at once, but prayerfully, day by day by day, relying on Him faithfully, we will see our lives transformed. So much so that people will take notice. Our husbands will praise us. And our children will rise up and call us blessed!

Holy Spirit, I want to be the kind of woman my kids can admire and imitate. Help me resist being intimidated by Proverbs 31 and find encouragement and inspiration instead. Amen. —AH

In Our Time of Need

Let us then approach God's throne of grace with confidence, so that
we may receive mercy and find grace to help us in our time of need.
HEBREWS 4:16

*H*as your child ever taken a flying leap into your arms? She is obviously confident that you will catch her. Has she called out to you when she's skinned her knee, assured that you will be there with a bandage, a tissue to wipe her tears, and a hug to make it all better? Or has she shared her deepest fears and nightmares, knowing that you will understand? It's very clear that your little girl has grown to trust you. She knows you love her and you understand.

That is the kind of trust we can bring to God, only He is worthy of a greater faith since He has promised in His Word that He will never leave us or fail us. We can leap into our heavenly Father's arms with complete confidence that He will catch us. That He will be there when we've fallen. That He will hear that cry in the night. That He will understand our deepest fears. That in His everlasting arms we will find hope, healing, comfort, mercy, forgiveness, and a love that endures forever.

We can rest there, knowing we've truly come to the right place in our time of need.

Let us pray that we can come to trust the Lord in such a way. And that our children will learn that same kind of trust in Him.

His arms are ever waiting.

Heavenly Father, thank You for accepting me with wide-open arms, ready to protect, comfort, and heal. You are always near in my time of need. Amen. —AH

One of His Promises

Then you will call on me and come and pray to me, and I will listen to you.
JEREMIAH 29:12

It happens like this—you're at a function for ladies. A tea or luncheon. And within an hour, the aviary dynamics commence. To be heard above the twittering, the women get louder and chirpier and squawkier until the café is like a birdcage of pure noise. Sure, there might be some good laughs and some camaraderie, but deep down it makes you wonder—is anybody really listening in all that giddy brouhaha? Do you sometimes go home lonelier than you were before? And what about all those hours of social media? Are you really connecting with people in a profound and meaningful way? Enough that you feel loved and cared for when you shut off the computer?

Maybe there are days when you'd like for people to be quiet and just listen. Really hear you out. Know how you feel about what's happening in your world. To be heard, really heard and understood. Doesn't that sound good?

We have that caring attention in Christ. Every moment of every day. It's one of His promises to us. In fact, He is the greatest listener this rickety-rackety world will ever know. Let us use His gift with anticipation and with joy!

God, how wonderful that You listen to all my prayers—both spoken and unspoken. This is not something to be taken for granted but to be cherished and prized. Amen. —AH

Great Expectations!

*"Call to me and I will answer you and tell you great
and unsearchable things you do not know."*
JEREMIAH 33:3

People are more than a little bit intrigued with the wonders and phenomena of this world. Or with anything that seems mysterious or supernatural. Now why is that?

Lots of reasons, but one might be that it reminds us that there's something beyond us—*Someone* beyond us who is in control of this vast universe—and that fact brings us tremendous comfort.

God's mysteries are infinite and unfathomable, but when we approach Him with a humble spirit and a stillness in our souls, we may come away with sacred insights. His wisdom awaits us. His comfort and friendship. His corrections and guidance. His love. Great and unsearchable things may be illuminated before us. Perhaps the Holy Spirit will reveal more of His divine nature to us. Or offer us healing. Perhaps He would allow us to experience another dimension of His devotion to us or the sensations of heaven or the radiance of His holy presence? Even if in our devotion time we only come away with peace for the day, isn't that a supernatural wonder all by itself, considering this bustling world shouts of tranquility but knows little of it?

Connecting with our Lord in prayer is a worthy pursuit, and it will make motherhood that much more wonderful. Let us approach His throne with great expectations!

Holy Spirit, often I give lip service to Your supernatural power but my heart
does not truly believe. Ignite in me a radical, life-changing faith. Amen. —AH

What Is Love?

Love is patient, love is kind. It does not envy, it does not boast, it is not proud.
It does not dishonor others, it is not self-seeking, it is not easily angered, it keeps
no record of wrongs. Love does not delight in evil but rejoices with the truth.
It always protects, always trusts, always hopes, always perseveres.
1 CORINTHIANS 13:4–7

We get bombarded with the word *love* in the media and in movies and magazines. They show it. They crave it, manipulate it, and then rake it in like chips at a casino table. The marketplace is saturated with the word. They abuse it, twist it for their own purposes, and confuse it for the other *l* word—*lust.*

On and on and on until we are weary of the word. But what does God say about love?

In this brief passage from 1 Corinthians, we see that *love* was meant to be a noble word full of God's goodness and blessing. It's a word full of cherishing sensibilities and compassion and courage. God's love is the kind that considers others first and concentrates on the giving and not the getting.

How do we love those around us, including our children? Let's pray it looks like the kind of love God offers. After all, His love comes in its purest form, and it is beautiful to behold.

Lord, You are the author of perfect love. Help me accept the outpouring of Your love so that it might overflow into my interactions with others. Amen. —AH

Whatever You Wish

"If you remain in me and my words remain in you,
ask whatever you wish, and it will be done for you."
JOHN 15:7

When we read scriptures that tell us we can have anything we wish for, it's hard not to think of Santa Claus and our little Johnny with his long wish list for Christmas. There's the toy fire truck, of course. The one that lets out a whistle shrill enough to trigger a migraine. He's sure he *needs* the latest action figures—all the ones his friends have and some they don't so he'll have bragging rights. A game, but not the board kind. No clothes. Whatsoever. But maybe some serious cash. Hey, kids are savvy.

But having that Santa Claus way of thinking when we pray isn't what the scripture mean when we approach God with our requests or teach our kids to pray.

Then how are we to consider the various scriptures that tell us, "Ask and it will be given to you?" First, when we read all the scriptures on this topic we realize that there is an important caveat which concerns our perspective. If we stay near God and we stay grounded in His Word—so much so that it becomes a part of us—then we will naturally ask for things that will line up with scripture. We will ask for things that are pleasing to Him. And won't some of those answers to prayer bring us delight? Of course. God loves to give good gifts to His children.

How will the full meaning of these passages change the focus of your prayers today?

Lord, may the desires of my heart be pleasing to You.
Keep me aligned with Your holy will. Amen. —AH

Please Pass the Love!

Your love has given me great joy and encouragement, because you,
brother, have refreshed the hearts of the Lord's people.
PHILEMON 1:7

Do you ever wonder—how will your kids remember you when they are all grown up and gone?

What scenes will play out in their heads when they think of you? Will they remember you serving a sunny-side-up smile with their eggs or a side of crab? If it was ever the latter, you probably discovered that grouchiness is more than a little contagious. Kids learn quickly how to snap as sharp as a box turtle on the nose. Yikes!

Then again, maybe they will remember you with an upbeat attitude. A mom who knew how to laugh at herself. A mom who was never too busy to play, nourish, hug, help, challenge, inspire, and encourage. A mom who told them about Jesus, taught them to pray, and faithfully took them to church. And a mom who loved with her whole heart. It's hard for kids not to emulate this loving way of life. After all, love is more than a little contagious, too!

So, let us pray for more love. That we can give it away lavishly and accept it back with open arms. After all, that is just the way God loves you and me.

Father, help me be a loving example for my children, even when I'm annoyed, tired, or discouraged. When they think of me, I want them to see You working in my life. Amen. —AH

The Way They Should Go

Start children off on the way they should go,
and even when they are old they will not turn from it.
PROVERBS 22:6

*E*ven when our kids grow up and leave the house, our hearts go with them. Can't help it. We're not just Mom to our kids when they're born, we will always be their mom.

But kids have a way of becoming independent as they grow up. Some of that stretching outside of boundaries is perfectly normal as well as necessary. But sometimes a child or young person will stray in ways that become unhealthy. You say you trained her up right. Told her about Jesus and brought her to Christ. Helped her to follow Him by reading His Word, memorizing scriptures, attending Sunday school, and teaching her to pray.

And yet now in her exploration of new territories, she's decided to go the way of the world. What to do? Pray that your child will remember her training all those years growing up. That she will remember the way she should go. The way that will not bring destruction but peace and joy. In your prayers, remind God of His promise in Proverbs that says, "Start children off on the way they should go, and even when they are old they will not turn from it."

God, please draw my child back to You. Remind her of Your grace and Your ability to fulfill as nothing else can. Amen. —AH

Our Prayers Matter!

Therefore confess your sins to each other and pray for each other so that you may be healed. The prayer of a righteous person is powerful and effective.
JAMES 5:16

Hmmm. What do I need today? Actually, I have quite a long list to present to God."

That is right and good, but how much of that list includes others? Does your coworker need help in his marriage? Does your friend need comfort in grieving the loss of her mother? Does your dad need healing from a stroke? Do your kids need to learn to forgive? What about praying for the neighbors down the street? The pastor and elders in your congregation? How about praying for our nation's leaders and our president?

Guess our prayer list just got way longer, but this is how God wants us to pray, along with presenting our own needs to Him.

And as James 5:16 also reminds us—our prayers matter. A righteous person's prayer is effective and powerful! That scripture should bring us not only encouragement but a sense of urgency in our prayer life. Do you worry that you're not righteous enough? Then pray about that, too. God would surely be pleased if we asked Him to make us into virtuous women and mothers.

Lord, help me be sincere and persistent in my prayers—
not just when praying about myself but when I'm praying for others.
Give me a caring, compassionate heart. Amen. —AH

Help My Unbelief!

*But when you ask, you must believe and not doubt, because the one
who doubts is like a wave of the sea, blown and tossed by the wind.*
JAMES 1:6

𝒟id you read this scripture and then think, "Uh-oh—they're talking about me when they say not to doubt after you pray? Guess I'm the person who's getting blown to bits by the wind and sea with all my qualms and quailing."

We've all been guilty of succumbing to disbelief even after our most fervent prayer. But when you think about it, questioning the Almighty is a bit unproductive, not to mention dishonoring of the One who knows us best and loves us most. To wonder whether or not the Lord is going to answer our prayers in the right way— our way, of course—is common and human, but maybe it's a little like shrugging our shoulders at His tender mercies. Like forgetting those answered prayers—miracles seen and unseen. All those gifts given even when we forgot to ask.

When we pray we will be heard and we will receive an answer. It just may not be the answer we want or when we want it. In fact, the answer to our prayers, whatever they might be, may not come in our lifetimes, but in our home-going to heaven.

Maybe a good scripture to memorize is from Mark 9:24 that reads, "I do believe; help me overcome my unbelief!"

God, give me a bold, childlike faith. I don't want to be tossed by the wind;
I want to stand firm in You. Amen. —AH

How Do I Love Thee?

And I pray that you, being rooted and established in love, may have power, together with all the Lord's holy people, to grasp how wide and long and high and deep is the love of Christ.

Ephesians 3:17–18

Don't we all love Elizabeth Barrett Browning's sonnet, "How Do I Love Thee?" Here's the opening:

> *How do I love thee? Let me count the ways.*
> *I love thee to the depth and breadth and height*
> *My soul can reach, when feeling out of sight*

Ahh, we all wish someone would care about us so dearly, treasure us so sweetly, and be devoted to us so completely. Well, we are loved by God even beyond Elizabeth Barrett Browning's beautiful words.

To give up your life for your beloved is the greatest gift and the most profound sacrifice anyone can offer. And that is exactly what Jesus did for us. He faced torture and death that we might know life for all time. Perhaps we've heard the Easter story so many times we've become complacent. But our Lord's sacrifice was real, and it was a heavy price to pay. Imagine. It was all for love. And it was for us.

So, how does God love thee? Very well indeed!

The next time we pray, let us fully embrace that divine love with all our hearts and then let us offer it to our children who need to know that kind of love all the days of their lives and on into eternity.

Jesus, thank You for your boundless, sacrificial love. There is nothing that can separate me from that love. Amen. —AH

A Spiritual Hug

Praise be to the God and Father of our Lord Jesus Christ, the Father of compassion and the God of all comfort, who comforts us in all our troubles, so that we can comfort those in any trouble with the comfort we ourselves receive from God.

2 CORINTHIANS 1:3–4

What are the images that come to mind when you think of the ultimate comfort—especially after you've been weighted down with this thing called life? What would bring you a sense of well-being, relaxation, and general coziness?

Maybe being hugged by an overstuffed couch? Perhaps homemade chicken potpie hot out of the oven? How about slipping under some Egyptian cotton sheets with a down pillow for your head? Or a foot massage at a local spa with a little lavender aroma therapy thrown in? Then there's always that cuddly embrace from someone you love. Don't your shoulders relax at the thoughts of these kinds of special comforting delights?

Now think about the inspirational refreshment that comes from an intimate prayer time with God. Those precious moments with the Savior can become a far greater comfort to us than anything we can conjure up.

Then once we've absorbed that spiritual hug from above, maybe we can pass on that comfort to our kids, since they will be weighted down with the troubles of life, too.

Lord, help me run to You first whenever I'm overwhelmed. You are the ultimate comforter, whose embrace brings peace beyond understanding. Amen. —AH

Pinky Promise

Let us hold unswervingly to the hope we profess,
for he who promised is faithful.
HEBREWS 10:23

When you were a little girl did you ever make a pinky promise with one of your little gal friends? Did she keep her promise? Maybe. Maybe not. Promises are easy to make—but they are much harder to keep.

As adults, people still keep making lots of promises, but they go far beyond those pinkies. We've all heard, "The check is in the mail," "Your job is secure, "I've got your back," "This is the finest preowned car on the lot," "This supplement is like the fountain of youth," "I will love you and cherish you forever and always."

But people fail us. They give us their assurances, but too many times either their claims turn out to be deliberately bogus or they simply can't fulfill what they agreed upon because of circumstances out of their control. Either way, it's still a broken vow.

That is not the way of our Lord. If He makes a promise, He keeps it. And He has proven it so through the ages! We can cling to that hope. God is good, and He is faithful. Knowing this truth all the way to our souls will make prayer time that much more hope-filled. That much more stirring and splendid.

No more pinky promises. God is in control.

Father, You are a good and faithful God, worthy of my devotion and trust. Remind me daily of the hope I can find in the promises You have made. Amen. —AH

Like a Butterfly

"Watch and pray so that you will not fall into temptation.
The spirit is willing, but the flesh is weak."
MATTHEW 26:41

Temptations sometimes fly into our lives as innocently as a butterfly lighting on our shoulder. Other times temptations arrive as fast and as intense as a runaway truck barreling down a mountain. Either way, it's scary. No matter how temptation arrives, we have to be ready for it.

What tempts you? Is it that triple-layer chocolate cake on the kitchen counter that begs you to gobble up three pieces even though you know your cholesterol is through the roof? Or is it binge-watching a series on TV when your child really hoped you were going to help him with a science project? Or could it be carelessly cruel words tossed out to your family when you knew you should be more encouraging or patient?

Sin may seem to be an easy route at first, but it will inevitably bring us to a miserable place. A place we don't want to be.

So, how do we overcome when the spirit is willing, but the flesh is weak?

Stay watchful and pray. Ask the Lord to give you discernment when life gets confusing, to infuse you with the courage to stand against the enemy, and then to have the supernatural strength to overcome it!

God, instill in me a desire to live a holy life. Obeying You is the
only way to an abundant, joy-filled existence. Amen. —AH

That Wonderful Feeling

*In the morning, LORD, you hear my voice; in the morning
I lay my requests before you and wait expectantly.*
PSALM 5:3

Oh, that word—*expectant*—it's glorious, isn't it? Makes one think of babies arriving. Or maybe looking forward to the earth bursting forth with spring blossoms. Or perhaps watching a dream coming true before your eyes. Yes, expectation, it's that feeling of anticipation—when our hearts are full of hope—that life will bring us good things and a season of rejoicing!

You've seen the same eagerness when your child gazes up at you with that look of wondrous excitement, knowing full well you are about to give her all that was promised.

That is just the same way we are to pray—with a heart full of wondrous expectation.

Matthew 7:11 tells us, "If you, then, though you are evil, know how to give good gifts to your children, how much more will your Father in heaven give good gifts to those who ask him!" And He does want to give us good gifts, they just may not be the gifts we're begging for or the gifts we think will make our lives perfect. But rest assured, they will be the gifts we need.

If there was a choice, wouldn't we choose the gifts that God chooses for us? And wouldn't knowing that truth make our prayer time that much more expectant?

Holy Spirit, help me rejoice in the gifts You've given. And teach me to
wait in eager expectation for the blessings yet to come. Amen. —AH

The Snob Factor

"The Pharisee stood by himself and prayed: 'God, I thank you that I am not like other people—robbers, evildoers, adulterers—or even like this tax collector."
LUKE 18:11

Everyone is guilty of snobbery. Everyone. Even our prayers can be riddled with that particular prickly offense. But it's not a good way to be or to pray. God is not amused with a haughty attitude. In fact, He detests it.

This passage of scripture, which is provided here from Luke, shows us how we shouldn't pray. There can be no misunderstandings. The Lord does not like the Pharisee's style of prayer—which was full of pomp and false piety. This Pharisee even had the audacity to remind God how much holier he was than the other people around him by saying, "'I fast twice a week and give a tenth of all I get.' But the tax collector stood at a distance. He would not even look up to heaven, but beat his breast and said, 'God, have mercy on me, a sinner.' I tell you that this man, rather than the other, went home justified before God. For all those who exalt themselves will be humbled, and those who humble themselves will be exalted" (Luke 18:12–14).

It was the tax collector, praying with humility and genuine repentance who was given praise and favor. He would be exalted. What a difference in the two prayers and the unexpected outcome for both men.

May we all pray as the tax collector!

God, break down my pride and self-righteousness. I want to come before You on my knees, with a spirit of true humility. Amen. —AH

When We Bow Our Heads

For there is one God and one mediator between
God and mankind, the man Christ Jesus.
1 TIMOTHY 2:5

We live in a world of many gods. They're everywhere. They're even showing up at the local department stores, masquerading as décor, and people are happy to buy them and put them in a place of honor in their homes. These days, people worship just about everything, including trees, money, fame, you name it. And hey, they worship themselves when their belief system promises that they, too, will be gods someday. Pretty enticing religion, eh?

But the Bible tells us that there is only one God. And there is only one mediator between God and mankind.

His name is Jesus.

In John 14:6 Jesus said, "I am the way and the truth and the life. No one comes to the Father except through me."

So, may we never get confused about whom we are praying to. Not to a nebulous deity. Not a god that man cooked up with the help of demonic influences. Not nature or material things or ourselves. We are praying to God, in Jesus' name. The only One who is worthy of our worship and our praise!

Lord, root out any idols that might be lurking in my heart. Don't let me get distracted by all the false altars of worship this world has to offer. The only God I want to exalt is You. Amen. —AH

Sweet Music to God's Ears

One of them, when he saw he was healed, came back, praising God in a loud voice.
He threw himself at Jesus' feet and thanked him—and he was a Samaritan.
Jesus asked, "Were not all ten cleansed? Where are the other nine? Has no one
returned to give praise to God except this foreigner?" Then he said to him,
"Rise and go; your faith has made you well."
LUKE 17:15–19

We would all like to know more about the nature of God, wouldn't we? Luke gives us another facet of His divine character in chapter 17.

It's obvious in this short passage that Jesus appreciates a grateful heart. He'd healed ten lepers, but only one came back to give thanks to the Lord. Did the other men get so excited they forgot to thank the Lord as they ran willy-nilly to find their family and friends? Did they not really care where the healing had come from but only cared that they were clean and could rejoin their communities? What could have been their motivation for such rudeness? We don't know the rest of the story, but we do know that one man did please the Lord by coming back to show his gratitude.

We are careful to teach our children to say please and thank you, but have we told them that when the Lord answers our prayers we should say, "Thank you, Jesus"?

Words of gratitude and praise to our Lord must surely be like sweet music to His ears.

Jesus, Your words convict me. Forgive me for not thanking You with a grateful spirit every day. You have given me so much that I take for granted. Amen. —AH

About the Authors

*B*estselling and award-winning author **Anita Higman** has over forty books published (several coauthored) for adults and children. She's been a Barnes & Noble "Author of the Month" for Houston and has a BA degree, combining speech communication, psychology, and art. Anita loves good movies, exotic teas, and brunch with her friends.

Marian Leslie is a writer and freelance editor. She has lived in southwestern Ohio most of her days, but has ventured far and wide through the pages of many good books. This is Marian's third collaboration with her good friend and writing partner, Anita.